W9-CAF-794

Developmental Psychology

By George Zgourides, Psy.D.

IDG
BOOKS
WORLDWIDE

IDG Books Worldwide, Inc.
An International Data Group Company
Foster City, CA ♦ Chicago, IL ♦ Indianapolis, IN ♦ New York, NY

About the Author

George Zgourides, Psy.D., is a licensed clinical psychologist specializing in anxiety, phobias, sexuality, Traditional Chinese Medicine (TCM) approaches to healing, and the sociology of religion. His academic appointments have included Assistant Professor of Psychology at the University of Portland (Portland, Oregon), Associate Professor of Psychology and Sociology at New Mexico Military Institute (Roswell, New Mexico), and Academic Dean at the Dallas Institute of Acupuncture and Oriental Medicine (Dallas, Texas).

Publisher's Acknowledgments

Editorial

Editors: Linda S. Stark, Ellen Considine

Acquisitions Editor: Kris Fulkerson

Production

Proofreader: Paula Lowell

IDG Books Indianapolis Production Department

CliffsQuickReview™ Developmental Psychology

Published by
IDG Books Worldwide, Inc.
An International Data Group Company
919 E. Hillsdale Blvd.
Suite 400
Foster City, CA 94404

www.idgbooks.com (IDG Books Worldwide Web site)
www.cliffsnotes.com (CliffsNotes Web site)

Library of Congress Control Number: 00-104209

ISBN: 0-7645-8614-9

Printed in the United States of America

10 9 8 7 6 5 4 3 2 1

1O/RS/QX/QQ/IN

Distributed in the United States by IDG Books Worldwide, Inc.

Distributed by CDG Books Canada Inc. for Canada; by Transworld Publishers Limited in the United Kingdom; by IDG Norge Books for Norway; by IDG Sweden Books for Sweden; by IDG Books Australia Publishing Corporation Pty. Ltd. for Australia and New Zealand; by TransQuest Publishers Pte Ltd. for Singapore, Malaysia, Thailand, Indonesia, and Hong Kong; by Gotop Information Inc. for Taiwan; by ICG Muse, Inc. for Japan; by Intersoft for South Africa; by Eyrolles for France; by International Thomson Publishing for Germany, Austria and Switzerland; by Distribuidora Cuspide for Argentina; by LR International for Brazil; by Galileo Libros for Chile; by Ediciones ZETA S.C.R. Ltda. for Peru; by WS Computer Publishing Corporation, Inc., for the Philippines; by Contemporanea de Ediciones for Venezuela; by Express Computer Distributors for the Caribbean and West Indies; by Micronesia Media Distributor, Inc. for Micronesia; by Chips Computadoras S.A. de C.V. for Mexico; by Editorial Norma de Panama S.A. for Panama; by American Bookshops for Finland.

For general information on IDG Books Worldwide's books in the U.S., please call our Consumer Customer Service department at **800-762-2974**. For reseller information, including discounts and premium sales, please call our Reseller Customer Service department at **800-434-3422**.

For information on where to purchase IDG Books Worldwide's books outside the U.S., please contact our International Sales department at **317-596-5530** or fax **317-572-4002**.

For consumer information on foreign language translations, please contact our Customer Service department at **1-800-434-3422**, fax 317-572-4002, or e-mail rights@idgbooks.com.

For information on licensing foreign or domestic rights, please phone **+1-650-653-7098**.

For sales inquiries and special prices for bulk quantities, please contact our Order Services department at **800-434-3422** or write to the address above.

For information on using IDG Books Worldwide's books in the classroom or for ordering examination copies, please contact our Educational Sales department at **800-434-2086** or fax **317-572-4005**.

For press review copies, author interviews, or other publicity information, please contact our Public Relations department at **650-653-7000** or fax **650-653-7500**.

For authorization to photocopy items for corporate, personal, or educational use, please contact Copyright Clearance Center, 222 Rosewood Drive, Danvers, MA 01923, or fax **978-750-4470**.

What Is Developmental Psychology?

Developmental psychology is the scientific study of age-related changes throughout the human life span. A discipline of scientific inquiry, developmental psychology recognizes humans of all societies and cultures as beings who are "in process," or constantly growing and changing. This discipline identifies the biological, psychological, and social aspects that interact to influence the growing human life-span process. Beginning with Sigmund Freud (1856–1939) and Jean Piaget (1896–1980), the early focus of developmental psychology was on **child development,** or the maturation of children. Within the last 25 years, **developmentalists**—researchers who study human development—expanded their focus to include the study of the physical, motor, cognitive, intellectual, emotional, personality, social, and moral changes that occur throughout all stages of the life span.

Issues in Developmental Psychology

Two of the more highly debated issues in life-span development psychology today are continuity versus discontinuity and nature versus nurture.

At the heart of the **continuity versus discontinuity** debate lies the question of whether development is solely and evenly continuous, or whether it is marked by age-specific periods. Developmentalists who advocate the **continuous model** describe development as a relatively smooth process, without sharp or distinct stages, through which an individual must pass. Meanwhile, supporters of the **discontinuous model** describe development as a series of discrete **stages,** each of which is characterized by at least one task that an individual must accomplish before progressing to the next stage. For example, Freud,

in his stage model of **psychosexual development,** theorized that children systematically move through oral, anal, phallic, and latency stages before reaching mature adult sexuality in the genital stage. Theories of human development, according to Freud and Erikson, appear in Table 1-1. Table 1-2 shows Piaget's stages of cognitive development, and Table 1-3 outlines Levinson's stages of passage from age 17 to 65 and over.

Table 1-1: Theories of Developmental Stages, per Freud and Erikson

Period (Age)	Freud's Stages	Erikson's Task or Crisis
Infancy (0–1)	Oral	Trust vs. mistrust
Toddlerhood and early childhood (1–3)	Anal	Autonomy vs. shame
Early childhood (3–6)	Phallic	Initiative vs. guilt
Middle childhood (7–11)	Latency	Industry vs. inferiority
Adolescence (12–19)	Genital	Identity vs. confusion
Early adulthood (20–45)		Intimacy vs. isolation
Middle adulthood (45–65)		Generativity vs. stagnation
Late adulthood (65+)		Integrity vs. despair

Table 1-2: Piaget's Stages of Cognitive Development

Stage	Age	Characteristics of Stage
Sensorimotor	0–2	The child learns by doing: looking, touching, sucking. The child also has a primitive understanding of cause-and-effect relationships. Object permanence appears around 9 months.
Preoperational	2–7	The child uses language and symbols, including letters and numbers. Egocentrism is also evident. Conservation marks the end of the preoperational stage and the beginning of concrete operations.
Concrete Operations	7–11	The child demonstrates conservation, reversibility, serial ordering, and a mature understanding of cause-and-effect relationships. Thinking at this stage is still concrete.
Formal Operations	12+	The individual demonstrates abstract thinking, including logic, deductive reasoning, comparison, and classification.

Table 1-3: Levinson's Theory of Human Development

Age	Stage
17–33	Novice phase of early adulthood
17–22	Early adult transition
22–28	Entering the adult world
28–33	Age-30 transition
33–45	Culmination of early adulthood
33–40	Settling down
40–45	Midlife transition
45–50	Entering middle adulthood
50–55	Age-50 transition
55–60	Culmination of middle adulthood
60–65	Late adult transition
65+	Late adulthood

Proponents of stage theories of development also suggest that individuals go through **critical periods,** which are times of increased and favored sensitivity to particular aspects of development. For example, early childhood (the first 5 years) is a critical period for language acquisition. Thus, most adults find it difficult or impossible to master a second language during their adult years while young children raised in bilingual homes normally learn second languages easily during childhood.

Experts from a variety of disciplines continue to argue over the roles that biology and the environment ultimately play in development. This centuries-old **nature-versus-nurture** debate concerns the relative degree to which heredity and learning affect functioning. Both genetic traits and environmental circumstances are likely to be involved in an individual's development, although the amount each express depends on the individual and his or her circumstances. For example, some identical twins who are separated at birth develop similar personality, cognitive, and social characteristics, while other twins who are separated at birth do not. Likewise, many non-twin siblings raised in the same household develop similar characteristics, although this similar development of characteristics is not always the case with non-twin siblings. This interactional nature-versus-nurture or biology-versus-environment approach to the study of human psychological development exemplifies the multifaceted makeup of the biopsychosocial perspective.

The Biopsychosocial Perspective of Developmental Psychology

The interaction of biological, psychological, and social aspects of developmental psychology form the essence of the holistic **biopsychosocial perspective.** The biopsychosocial perspective attributes complex phenomena or events to multiple causes. Figure 1-1 shows the interrelationship of the fields of study that constitute the biopsychosocial perspective. In contrast to the biopsychosocial perspective is the **reductionistic perspective,** which reduces complex phenomenon or events to a single cause.

Figure 1-1

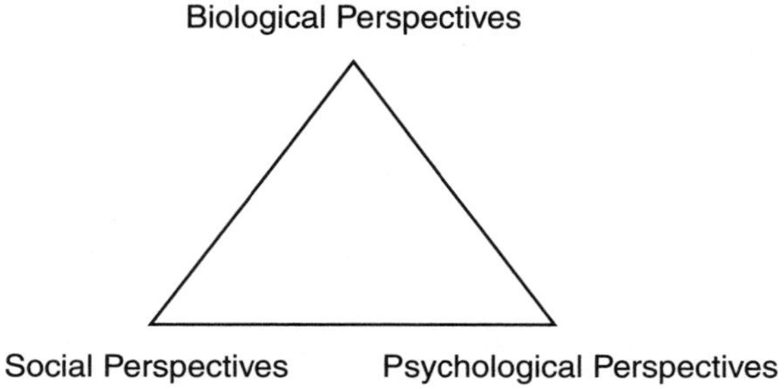

Biological Perspectives

Social Perspectives   Psychological Perspectives

This biopsychosocial model of developmental psychology may be applied to the case of John, a depressed adolescent male, who finds it difficult to socialize with his peers. John's problem may be the result of any one of a number of causes. For example, **injunctions,** or messages received during childhood, may be considered one possible cause of John's depression. Injunctions may include messages regarding worthlessness and shame, distorted perceptions, fears of rejection, and inadequate communication and social skills. John's overly critical parents raised him to believe that he would never amount to anything or have any friends. As John experiences distress over his negative injunctions about relationships (psychological), he "tries too hard" to make others like him, which causes his peers to distance themselves from him (social). In time, John may experience rejection and become more depressed (psychological). Berating himself (psychological), John may become less concerned with his outward appearance and hygiene (biological), which in turn may cause his peers to avoid further contact with him (social).

For obvious reasons, developmental psychologists are cognizant of these types of interacting biological, psychological, and social components when considering life-span events and issues. In a case such as John's, a developmentalist may choose to conceptualize and treat his problem from all three perspectives, rather than focusing on one. Because of the developmentalist's method of exploring all three perspectives, John benefits from a holistic and comprehensive approach to his difficulties.

Research Concepts in Developmental Psychology

Whether or not a particular discipline, such as psychology, is a science has more to do with the methods used than with the particular subject area studied. An area of inquiry is a scientific discipline if its investigators use the **scientific method**—a systematic approach to researching questions and problems through objective and accurate observation, collection and analysis of data, direct experimentation, and replication of these procedures. Scientists emphasize the importance of gathering information carefully and accurately, and researchers strive to remain unbiased when evaluating information, observing phenomena, conducting experiments, and recording procedures and results. Researchers also recognize the value of skepticism and the necessity of having their findings confirmed by other scientists.

Developmental psychology research is the scientific means of acquiring information about groups and individuals regarding various aspects of human development. A developmental psychologist begins a research study after developing ideas from a **theory,** or an integrated set of statements, that explain various phenomena. Because a theory is too general to test, the investigator devises a **hypothesis**—a testable prediction—from the theory and tests the hypothesis instead of a general theory. The results of the research study either disprove or do not disprove the hypothesis. If the hypothesis is disproved, it cannot be used to make predictions, and the investigator must question the accuracy of the theory. If the hypothesis is not disproved, the scientist can use it to make predictions about the phenomena that he or she is studying. These predictions may help scientists do one of the following:

- Form explanations of the causes of the phenomena.
- Draw conclusions about how the phenomena will affect groups and individuals.

A goal of developmental research is to discover the developmental similarities, differences, patterns, and trends of the **population** group that is under investigation. A population is a body of persons having qualities or characteristics in common. Members of a population who participate in a study are referred to as **subjects** or **respondents.** When the characteristics of a portion of the population are representative of the characteristics of the entire population, scientists can apply, or **generalize,** their findings from the **sample** to the population as a whole. The best and most representative sample is a **random sample,** in which each member of a population has an equal chance of being chosen as a subject.

In **quantitative research,** information is collected from respondents (for example, the number of years that they have been in college) and converted into numbers (junior equals 3; senior equals 4). In **qualitative research,** information collected from respondents takes the form of verbal descriptions or direct observations of events. Although verbal descriptions and observations are useful, many scientists prefer quantitative data for purposes of analysis.

When information is collected through a test, researchers try to ensure that the test is

- **Valid:** Measures what it purports to measure.

- **Reliable:** Provides consistent results when administered on different occasions.

To analyze data, scientists use mathematical procedures known as **statistics** to describe and draw inferences from data. Two types of statistics are most common:

- **Inferential:** used for making predictions about the population.

- **Descriptive:** used for describing the characteristics of the population and subjects. Scientists use both types of statistics to draw general conclusions about their population and sample.

Research Designs and Methods in Developmental Research

Researchers use many different designs and methods to study human development. The three most popular **designs** are

- **Cross-sectional:** a number of different-age individuals with the same trait or characteristic of interest are studied at a single time.

- **Longitudinal:** the same individuals are studied repeatedly over a specified period of time.

- **Cross-sequential:** individuals in a cross-sectional sample are tested more than once over a specified period of time.

Seven popular life-span research **methods** include the case study, survey, observational, correlational, experimental, cross-cultural, and participant observation methods.

Case-study research

In **case-study research,** an investigator studies an individual who has a rare or unusual condition or who has responded favorably to a new treatment. Case studies are typically clinical in scope. The investigator—often a physician, psychologist, social worker, counselor, or educator—interviews the subject, obtains background records, and administers questionnaires to acquire quantifiable data on the subject. A comprehensive case study can last months or years. Throughout the duration of the case study, the researcher documents the condition, treatment, and effects in relation to each patient and summarizes all of this information in individual **case reports.** A typical case report follows this format:

1. **Presenting problem:** The condition or problem.

2. **Case history:** A brief social history pertinent to the client's presenting problem.

3. **Treatment:** A description of the treatment process, including details from each session.

4. **Results of treatment:** A description of treatment effects, if any.

5. **Follow-up:** A description of the long-term treatment effects, if any.

Although case studies are valuable for obtaining useful information about individuals and rare conditions, they tend to focus on the pathology—the characteristics and effects of a particular disease—and are therefore applicable only to individuals with similar conditions rather than to the general population.

Survey research

Survey research involves interviewing or administering questionnaires or written surveys to large numbers of people. The investigator analyzes the data obtained from surveys to learn about similarities, differences, and trends, and then makes predictions about the population being studied. Advantages of survey research include the great amount of information the researcher can obtain from the large number of respondents, the convenience for respondents of taking a written survey, and the low cost of acquiring and processing data. Mail-in surveys have the added advantage of ensuring anonymity and thus prompting respondents to answer questions truthfully.

Disadvantages of survey research include volunteer bias, interviewer bias, and distortion. **Volunteer bias** occurs when a sample of volunteers is not representative of the general population. Subjects who are willing to talk about certain topics may answer surveys differently than those who are not. **Interviewer bias** occurs when an interviewer's expectations or insignificant gestures (such as frowning or smiling) inadvertently influence a subject's responses one way or the other. **Distortion** occurs when a subject does not respond honestly to questions.

Observational research

Because distortion can be a serious limitation of survey research, scientists may choose to observe subjects' behavior directly through **observational research.** Observational research takes place in either a laboratory **(laboratory observation)** or a natural setting **(naturalistic observation).** In either research method, observers record participants' behavior within an environment. Observational research reduces the possibility of subjects giving misleading accounts of their experiences, not taking the study seriously, being unable to remember details, or feeling too embarrassed to disclose everything that happened.

Observational research has limitations, however. Volunteer bias is common, because volunteers may not be representative of the general public. Individuals who agree to be observed and monitored may function differently than respondents who do not want to be observed and monitored. Individuals may also function differently in a laboratory setting than respondents who are observed in more-natural settings.

Correlational research

A developmentalist may also conduct **correlational research.** A **correlation** is a relationship between two **variables** (factors that change). Variables may include characteristics, attitudes, behaviors, or events. The goal of correlational research is to determine whether or not a relationship exists between two variables, and if a relationship does exist, the number of commonalities in that relationship. A researcher may use case-study methods, surveys, interviews, and observational research to discover correlations. Correlations are either positive (to +1.0), negative (to−1.0), or nonexistent (0.0). In a **positive correlation,** the values of the variables increase or decrease (co-vary) together. In a **negative correlation,** one variable increases as the other variable decreases. In a **nonexistent correlation,** there is no relationship between variables.

Although correlation is commonly confused with causation, correlational data does not indicate a cause-and-effect relationship. When a correlation is present, changes in the value of one variable reflect changes in the value of the other. The correlation does not imply that one variable causes the other variable, only that both variables are somehow related. To study the effects that variables have on each other, an investigator must conduct an experiment.

Experimental research

Experimental research is concerned with *how* and *why* something happens. The goal of experimental research is to test the effect that an **independent variable,** which the scientist manipulates, has on a **dependent variable,** which the scientist observes. In other words, experimental research leads to conclusions regarding causation.

A number of factors can affect the outcome of any type of experimental research. For instance, investigators face the challenge of finding samples that are random and representative of the population being studied. Additionally, researchers must guard against **experimenter bias,** in which their expectations about what should or should not happen in the study sway the results. Researchers should also control **extraneous variables,** such as room temperature or noise level, that may interfere with the results of the experiment. Only when experimenters carefully control extraneous variables can they draw valid conclusions about the effects of specific variables on other variables.

Cross-cultural research

Western cultural standards do not necessarily apply to other societies, and what may be normal or acceptable for one group may be abnormal or unacceptable for another group. Sensitivity to others' norms, folkways, values, mores, attitudes, customs, and practices necessitates knowledge of other societies and cultures. Developmentalists may conduct **cross-cultural research,** research designed to reveal variations existing across different groups of people. Most cross-cultural research involves survey, direct observation, and participant observation methods of research. The challenge of this type of research is to avoid experimenter bias and the tendency to compare dissimilar characteristics as if they were somehow related.

Participant observation

Participant observation requires an observer to become a member of his or her subjects' community. An advantage of this method of research is the opportunity to study what actually occurs within a community and then consider that information within the political, economic, social, and religious systems of that community. A disadvantage of participant observation is the problem of subjects altering their behavior because, as subjects of the observation, the participants know that they are being watched.

Research Ethics

Ethics are self-regulatory guidelines for making decisions and defining professions. By establishing ethical codes, professional organizations maintain the integrity of the profession, define the expected conduct of members, and protect the welfare of subjects and clients. Moreover, ethical codes give professionals direction when confronting confusing situations that are **ethical dilemmas.** A case in point is a scientist's decision to deceive subjects intentionally. On one hand, the scientist may believe that deception is the only way to conduct a particular study, while on the other hand, the scientist needs to be cognizant of and protect the subjects' right to their integrity and dignity.

Many organizations, such as the American Psychological Association, have ethical principles and guidelines to help scientists make responsible decisions in cases where ethical dilemmas arise. The vast majority of modern developmentalists abide by their respective organizations' ethical principles.

Researchers must remain mindful of their ethical responsibilities to participants and remember that their primary duty is to protect their subjects' welfare. For example, a researcher whose study requires extensive questioning of volunteers' personal information should screen the study's subjects beforehand to assure that the questioning is not distressing. Scientists should also inform subjects about their

expected roles in the study, the potential risks of participating, and their freedom to withdraw from the study at any time without consequences. Agreeing to participate in a study based on disclosure of personal information is known as **informed consent.** After the study is concluded, the researcher should **debrief** the subjects by providing the volunteers with the complete details of the study.

Many critics believe that the intentional use of **deception,** or concealing the purpose and procedures of a study from participants, is never justified. Deception carries the risk of psychologically harming subjects and also reduces public support for research. Proponents of deception in research, however, view it as necessary when prior knowledge of a study would sway a subject's responses and invalidate the results. For example, when subjects learn that the purpose of a study is to measure attitudes of racial discrimination, the participants may intentionally try to avoid appearing prejudiced.

Even the most ethical and cautious researcher cannot anticipate every risk associated with volunteers participating in a study. However, by carefully screening subjects, informing subjects of their rights, giving them as much information as possible before the study, avoiding deception, and debriefing the subjects after the study, researchers may at least minimize the risks of harm to their subjects.

Evaluating Developmental Research

Sources of developmental research—scholarly journals and books, national magazine surveys, television programs, and tabloids—vary considerably in the quality of information offered. Consequently, properly assessing research validity is important when studying developmental psychology. Poorly designed or conducted research tends to fuel society's misconceptions about developmental topics, such as the topic or myth that older adults are never interested in sex. While the media tend to present the elderly as asexual grandparent-types, this stereotype contradicts actual scientific research that shows nearly 90 percent of older-adult residents in nursing homes are sexually active.

Professional journals and periodicals are the most accurate sources of scientific information about life-span development. Professional researchers and clinicians contribute the majority of material to these journals, but their peers also review the material. Thus, the quality of the research published tends to be quite high. A few of the leading developmental journals include *Child Development, Children Today, Developmental Psychology, Family Life Educator, Family Relations, Journal of Gerontology, Journal of Marriage and Family,* and *Pediatrics.* Popular magazines and broadcast journalism generally do not provide accurate or scientific information about life-span development. Instead, studies reported in these media are usually sensationalistic and/or poorly designed.

Stages of Pregnancy

During a full-term human **pregnancy,** a fetus is carried in the uterus for a **gestation** period averaging 280 days from the last menstrual period until birth (266 days from conception to birth). The 280 days are frequently divided into 10 four-week **lunar months** of 28 days each, which equal slightly more than nine **calendar months,** as shown in Figure 3-1. Pregnancies are also often divided into **trimesters,** periods of three calendar months (13 weeks).

Figure 3-1

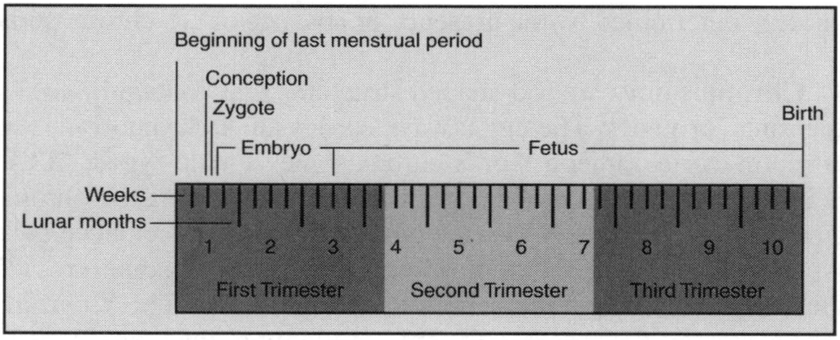

Conception

Around day 14 of a 28-day menstrual cycle, the average woman **ovulates** and releases an egg, or **ovum,** from one of her ovaries. The ovum is then picked up by fingerlike structures called **fimbriae** and is swept into the nearby **fallopian tube.** If **conception** occurs and a sperm and ovum unite, the newly formed **zygote,** or **conceptus,** travels down the fallopian tube and attaches to the uterine wall. If conception does not occur, the ovum dissolves in approximately 48 hours.

Sperm usually reach the egg in the portion of the fallopian tube closest to the ovary within 90 minutes after ejaculation. **Mitochondria** (tiny energy sources for cells) in the midpiece of sperm cause the tail of the sperm to lash about. This **flagellation,** or lashing out, propels the sperm through the woman's vagina and into her tubes. Of the average 300 million sperm present in each ejaculation, an estimated 2,000 eventually reach the fallopian tube containing the ovum. Only 50 sperm may actually reach the egg. The remaining sperm are either killed by the acidic environment of the vagina or by entering the wrong fallopian tube. Only one sperm penetrates and fertilizes the ovum. The others surround the egg and secrete the enzyme **hyaluronidase** to soften the gelatinous covering of the egg, the **zona pellucida.** Once penetrated, the ovum's surrounding membrane thickens to prevent other sperm from entering.

Fertilization is completed when the nucleus of the head of the sperm fuses with the nucleus of the egg. At this time, the sex of the zygote is determined by the presence or absence of a Y chromosome.

Chromosomes are rod-shaped structures that contain biological blueprints, or **genes.** The egg always carries an X chromosome, and the sperm carries either a Y or X chromosome. A male zygote (XY) is the product of the fusion of an egg with a sperm carrying a Y chromosome; a female zygote (XX) is the product of the fusion of an egg with a sperm carrying an X chromosome. The X chromosome provides valuable genetic material essential to life and health. The Y chromosome is smaller than the X and carries little more than directions for producing a male.

A **multiple pregnancy** occurs if two or more eggs are fertilized, or a single fertilized egg divides into two or more zygotes. Two embryos from a single egg develop into **identical twins;** three embryos develop into **identical triplets.** Two separate eggs fertilized by two sperm develop into **fraternal twins.**

Within 24 to 36 hours, the single-cell zygote begins dividing exponentially as it moves along the fallopian tube. One cell becomes two, two becomes four, four becomes eight, and so forth.

Implantation

Within a week after conception, the zygote becomes a **blastocyst,** or a hollow ball of about 100 cells, no larger than it was before cell division began. After floating in the uterus for about 3 days, the blastocyst attaches to the **endometrium,** or inner lining of the uterus. The outer cells of the blastocyst, or the **trophoblasts** (which form the trophectoderm), secrete enzymes that dissolve layers of uterine lining, allowing the blastocyst to firmly attach to the endometrium. This **implantation** occurs about a week after conception. After implantation, and for the first 8 weeks of gestation, the zygote is referred to as an **embryo.** (See Figure 3-2 for illustration of the early development of the embryo.) Following the first 8 weeks until birth, it is referred to as a **fetus.**

Figure 3-2

Uterus
Ovary
Ovulation
Fertilization
Fertilized egg
Zygote (24 hour)
Fallopian tube
Endometrium
Trophoblast (Day 6)
Inner cell mass
Two-cell stage (30 hour)
Four-cell stage (Day 2)
Morula (Day 3)
Blastocyst (Days 4-5)
Implantation of blastocyst (Day 7)
Inner cell mass
Endometrium

During implantation, the rate of cell division increases, and the first signs of specialized organs and tissues appear. For example, a small indentation, the **neural groove,** forms and later develops into the fetus's brain and nervous system. After implantation, other cells, including the trophoblasts, develop into the fetus's placenta, umbilical cord, and amniotic sac.

The **placenta** is a disk-shaped structure of tissue that forms along the uterine wall on one side and attaches to the fetus via the umbilical cord. The placenta's function is to pass oxygen, nourishment, and antibodies from the mother's blood to the developing fetus. Similarly, waste products from the fetus are passed to the mother for elimination. Early in gestation the placenta begins secreting the hormone **human chorionic gonadotropin (HCG).** HCG inhibits menstrual periods by preserving the **corpus luteum** (the empty Graafian follicle which releases the mature ovum) during the early stages of pregnancy. The hormone is present in a woman's blood and urine soon after conception and is the basis of most common pregnancy tests: If HCG is present, the test is positive, and the woman is pregnant. Home-based tests are more likely than laboratory tests to give **false negative** results, which may lead the woman to think she is not pregnant when she is. Thus, home pregnancy tests are not as reliable as laboratory tests.

Formed during the fifth week of embryonic development, the **umbilical cord** carries blood to and from the fetus via one vein and two arteries. Fetal blood circulates through the **chorionic villi,** which are small fingerlike projections in the placenta. The mother's and infant's circulatory systems remain totally separate, yet oxygen, carbon dioxide, waste products, nutrients, viruses, and assorted drugs can cross the membrane of the chorionic villi.

After the first trimester, the placenta also secretes large amounts of **progesterone** and **estrogen.** Many of the physical symptoms of pregnancy can be traced to the actions of these two hormones. Estrogen and progesterone stimulate enlargement of the reproductive organs and relaxation of associated ligaments, stimulate development of the uterine lining and mammary glands, and prevent contractions of the uterus. Another hormone produced by the placenta, **placental lactogen,** prepares the mammary glands to secrete milk.

Two membranes surround the embryo; the inner membrane is known as the **amnion,** and the outer membrane is called the **chorion.** The fetus floats in the waterlike **amniotic fluid** that fills the **amniotic sac** (formed from the fusion of the amnion and chorion). Amniotic fluid cushions the developing fetus against injury and shock and provides constant temperature in the amniotic sac.

The first trimester

When a woman suspects that she is pregnant, she should have her status confirmed as soon as possible. One method is to administer an HCG-based pregnancy test. Another is **ballottement,** a type of pelvic examination in which a physician or nurse feels for a fetus in the uterus. Pregnancy may also be verified when a doctor hears a fetal rushing sound, or **uterine souffle,** by listening through a stethoscope placed on the women's abdomen.

Fetal development occurs in **cephalocaudal** order, beginning with the head and ending with the lower body and extremities. This sequence of development results in the head of a typical fetus being disproportionately larger than the rest of its body.

Most of the fetus's systems and structures begin to form during the first 12 weeks of gestation. Three layers of cells differentiate to become the various body organs. The **ectoderm** (outermost layer) forms the sensory organs, skin, and nervous system. The **mesoderm** (middle layer) forms the connective tissues, muscles, skeleton, and circulatory and reproductive systems. The **endoderm** (innermost layer) forms the digestive, respiratory, and glandular systems.

The digestive and respiratory organs begin limited functioning by about week 7. The gonads have also already begun developing, even though fetus's gender is not yet externally visible.

The embryo weighs approximately $\frac{1}{30}$ of an ounce and is $1\frac{1}{4}$ inches long around week 8. The fetus's tongue, lips, ears, nose, and eyes can be seen. The fetus's head is much larger than the rest of its body due to rapid growth of the brain. Arms, hands, legs, feet, and toes are easily visible by week 10. The fetus looks like a tiny human, weighs approximately 1 ounce, is 3 or 4 inches long, and has discernible sex organs around week 12.

The second trimester

The second trimester begins with week 13. The mother can feel the movements of the 6-inch long fetus by about week 14. A physician can also detect a fetal heartbeat by weeks 17 or 18. Between weeks 20 and 26, the fetus may weigh as much as 2 pounds. The fetus's eyes are at now developed enough to open; at this point, the fetus sleeps, wakes, and moves its limbs.

The third trimester

The third trimester begins around week 27. The fetus now takes on a babylike appearance as a layer of fat forms beneath its skin. The fetus turns and assumes a head-down position in the womb as it prepares to enter the birth canal, or vagina. When a fetus does not turn, it is positioned feet-first or hips-first, and a **breech presentation** occurs.

By month 8, the fetus weighs about 5 pounds and gains $\frac{1}{2}$ pound each week thereafter. The fetus's skin becomes less reddish in color, and its wrinkles slowly disappear. A waxy material covers the fetus's skin to protect it during delivery.

Prenatal Care

All mothers-to-be should be concerned about prenatal care. Moderate exercise (such as walking), a wholesome diet, and avoidance of drugs and alcohol are essential for bringing a healthy baby into the world.

Drug use during pregnancy

Many chemicals pass easily from mother to fetus. Even seemingly harmless drugs like antihistamines and caffeine can cause fetal abnormalities, and what is a normal dosage of a drug for the mother may in fact be an overdose for the fetus. Such fetal sensitivity to drugs means that some common over-the-counter (OTC) medications (such as cold preparations, aspirin), prescription medications (such as antibiotics, steroids, opiates), and illegal/recreational drugs (such as marijuana, cocaine, heroin) are to be avoided. A variety of birth, or **congenital,** defects and deformities (deafness, absence of one or more limbs, mental retardation) can be traced to drug use during pregnancy. Drugs that cause visible fetal deformities are termed **teratogenic.**

The most common teratogens used by pregnant women include tobacco and alcohol. Women who smoke during pregnancy increase their risk of delivering a low birth weight, premature baby or of having a miscarriage. Women should completely avoid alcohol before and throughout pregnancy, because a level that determines heavy alcohol use is difficult to define. The amount of alcohol that causes **fetal alcohol syndrome,** which results in a congenital set of abnormalities (small head, low birth weight, unusual facial features, mental retardation), is also difficult to determine, but even amounts as small as two ounces a day have been shown to cause deformities.

Birthing alternatives

A woman has several choices regarding health care during her pregnancy. A new mother should decide as soon as possible whether or not she wants a physician, a **certified nurse midwife** (**CNM**), a hospital delivery or home delivery, and/or a medication-free delivery.

Many couples choose to take classes to prepare for childbirth. Perhaps the most popular childbirth preparation courses are classes on the **Lamaze method.** Lamaze classes consist of relaxation and controlled breathing training, as well as information on what to expect during labor and birth. The woman's partner is expected to participate in the labor process, serving as a labor coach. He or she assists by offering emotional support, helping the woman regulate her breathing, and keeping track of contractions.

Stages of Childbirth

Childbirth, or **parturition,** begins with **labor** (contractions of uterine muscles, opening of the cervix, and bearing down on the fetus) and concludes with **delivery** (expelling the baby and placenta from the vagina). Early signs of labor include short but mild contractions, blood-tainted vaginal discharge, and ruptured membranes (broken water).

The first stage of childbirth
The first stage of childbirth, or **labor,** typically lasts from 2 to 24 hours, depending on the number of previous deliveries. (In most cases, labor is longer for a first-time mother.) Regular contractions begin, and the cervix **dilates,** or opens up.

Labor occurs in three phases. During the **early phase,** mild, minute-long contractions occur every 15 minutes. During the **middle phase,** contractions increase in strength and frequency, and the cervix dilates to at least 2 or 3 inches. During the **late phase,** contractions become very painful, and the cervix dilates completely to about 10 cm, or 4 inches.

The second stage of childbirth

As contractions move the fetus through the birth canal, the woman may feel an urge to bear down and help expel the baby. By this time the cervix should be completely dilated. **Crowning** occurs when the baby's head can be seen at the vaginal orifice. In some cases, the baby presents hips or feet first. In such cases, the breech baby sometimes can be manually turned into a head-first position before delivery.

Once crowning begins, the woman may undergo an **episiotomy.** This procedure involves a physician making an incision in the **perineum** (the area between the vagina and anus) to prevent tearing as the baby moves through the vagina during birth.

The baby is delivered head and neck first, sometimes with the help of forceps. Upon delivery, the infant's mouth and nose are suctioned to prepare the baby's lungs to receive oxygen, and the umbilical cord is clamped and severed. Some physicians then gently pat the baby on the buttocks to initiate a breathing response. Drops of silver nitrate are administered to the newborn's eyes to prevent potential infection transmitted by the mother during birth.

A physician performs a **cesarean section (C-section)** when regular delivery of the child through the vagina is not recommended. To execute a C-section, the doctor makes an incision in the woman's lower abdomen, surgically opens the uterus, and removes the baby. Some reasons for C-sections include breech presentation, exceptionally difficult labor, disease (such as vaginal infection, herpes), and fetal distress.

The third stage of childbirth

During this final but short stage of childbirth, the placenta (the afterbirth) separates from the uterine wall and expels through the vagina. Before the physician repairs the episiotomy using stitches, it is important that the placenta is completely expelled. Infection and bleeding may occur when pieces of the placenta remain in the uterus.

The postpartum stage of childbirth

Bonding between the newborn and mother first takes place during the **postpartum** stage of childbirth. Many CNMs and physicians encourage the mother to hold her baby immediately after delivery to foster the bonding process. An infant who, for whatever reason, is separated from the mother at birth is not doomed to a life of emotional and mental difficulties. Immediate bonding is optimal, but infants can later make up for any problems resulting from initial separation.

A woman's hormone levels change dramatically after giving birth; in particular, the higher-than-usual levels of estrogen and progesterone suddenly decrease. These hormonal changes may be responsible, in part, for a new mother's **postpartum depression,** or baby blues. Postpartum depression can last from hours to months and may range in intensity from mild to severe.

Complications During Pregnancy and Childbirth

Numerous complications may arise during pregnancy and childbirth. These situations include **Rh factor incompatibility** (a mother with Rh– blood giving birth to a child with Rh+ blood), **ectopic pregnancy** (implantation outside of the uterus), **diabetes mellitus** (high blood sugar) **rubella** (German measles), and **eclampsia** (high blood pressure and fluid buildup).

Pregnant women also experience numerous minor symptoms during pregnancy. A frequent symptom is **morning sickness,** which is characterized by early-morning nausea, dizziness, and fatigue. The exact causes of morning sickness are unknown, but are probably due to hormonal changes in the woman's body. Such hormonal changes may also cause **chloasma,** or dark patches on the skin, which vanish early in postpartum. The **stretch marks** that appear on a woman's abdomen during pregnancy do not completely vanish but may turn lighter with time. Many pregnant women also suffer from stressed veins of the anus, or **hemorrhoids.** Hemorrhoids become uncomfortable as they itch, swell, or bleed.

Stillbirth and miscarriage

A **stillbirth** is the birth of a dead fetus after 20 weeks. A **miscarriage** is the spontaneous abortion of a **nonviable fetus** (one that is unable to live on its own) at less than 20 weeks gestation. Realistically, the number of miscarriages that occur every year is difficult to determine. As an example, a woman who does not realize she is pregnant may mistake a miscarriage for a menstrual period. Research, however, estimates that about 10 percent of pregnancies terminate in miscarriage. Chromosomal abnormalities are probably responsible for many miscarriages. In some cases, the ages of the mothers may also be a factor, as women over the age of 35 tend to have a higher incidence of miscarriages.

Premature birth

A **premature,** or preterm birth, a birth that occurs before a gestation of 37 weeks, differs from a stillbirth or a miscarriage in that the fetus is born **viable** (able to live outside of the uterus). Although many premature births are unexplained, some seem to be related to poor diet and alcohol or drug use during pregnancy, lack of prenatal care, and a history of premature births. The less an infant weighs at birth, the less chance it has of surviving.

Testing for disorders during pregnancy

Diagnostic tests are available for detecting potential fetal disorders and defects. An **ultrasound examination (sonogram)** involves bouncing high frequency sound waves off the fetus and transforming the bounced waves into visual images. During an **amniocentesis test,** a sample of the amniotic fluid is extracted by needle and is analyzed for fetal abnormalities such as fetal infections, chromosomal abnormalities, and other defects. Amniocentesis is performed no earlier than during week 15. Waiting until after week 15 helps the doctor avoid accidentally puncturing the fetus with the needle. Results of the amniocentesis are available within 1 to 2 weeks. **Chorionic villi sampling** tests for the same abnormalities as amniocentesis, though earlier (between weeks 9 and 14). In the placental covering are small **villi,** or thin blood-containing extensions. A physician performs a chorionic villi sampling by inserting a catheter into the uterus through the vagina. Then, a small amount of fluid is suctioned out through the catheter. Results for chorionic villi sampling are available within just a few days.

Infertility

Not all couples are able to conceive. A couple is said to be **infertile** after failing to conceive over a period of one or more years. As many as 20 percent of couples in the United States may be infertile. Approximately 65 percent of infertile couples eventually conceive without treatment.

Causes of male infertility include having too few mature sperm in the testes (below 20 million sperm per cubic centimeter of ejaculate), reduced sperm motility, failure to ejaculate into the vagina because of blocked sperm ducts or sexual dysfunction, and/or poor diet or health. Causes of female infertility include damaged or diseased reproductive organs, failure to ovulate regularly, blocked fallopian tubes, cervical mucous of incorrect consistency, growth of uterine tissue in the pelvic cavity, severe weight gain or loss, and/or poor diet or health.

Infertility is treated in a number of ways. **Fertility drugs,** ovulation-stimulating hormones, are used when infertility is due to the woman's inability to ovulate. The test-tube baby method, or **in vitro fertilization,** involves fertilizing an ovum and sperm outside the woman's body and implanting the embryo in the uterus. This procedure is often used when a woman's fallopian tubes are blocked. During **artificial insemination,** the man's sperm (or that of a donor) is collected and introduced into the woman's vagina via syringe. This technique may be especially valuable when a man's sperm count is below normal.

Most developmentalists divide childhood into **infancy** (birth to age 1), **toddlerhood** (ages 1 to 2), **early childhood** (ages 2 to 6), **middle childhood** (ages 7 to 11), and **adolescence** (ages 12 to 19).

Physical Development in Infancy and Toddlerhood

Infants and toddlers grow quickly; bodily changes are rapid and profound. **Physical development** refers to biological changes that children undergo as they age. Important aspects that determine the progress of physical development in infancy and toddlerhood include physical and brain changes; development of reflexes, motor skills, sensations, perceptions, and learning skills; and health issues.

The first 4 weeks of life are termed the **neonatal period.** Most babies weigh between 5 1/2 and 10 pounds, and are between 18 and 22 inches long. Male babies are generally slightly heavier and longer than female babies. Neonates born weighing less than 5 1/2 pounds are of **low birthweight.** Infants who arrive before their due date are **preterm** or **premature,** and these babies may or may not have a low birthweight. Babies who arrive on or shortly after their due date are **full-term.** Infants who arrive 2 or more weeks after their due date are **postmature.** Both premature and postmature babies are at higher risk of complications such as sickness, brain damage, or death, than are full-term babies.

Physical growth is especially rapid during the first 2 years. An infant's birthweight generally doubles by 6 months and triples by the infant's first birthday. Similarly, a baby grows between 10 and 12 inches in length (or height), and the baby's proportions change during the first 2 years. The size of an infant's head decreases in proportion from 1/3 of the entire body at birth, to 1/4 at age 2, to 1/8 by adulthood.

Fetal and neonatal brain developments are also rapid. The lower, or **subcortical,** areas of the brain (responsible for basic life functions, like breathing) develop first, followed by the higher areas, or **cortical** areas (responsible for thinking and planning). Most brain changes occur prenatally and soon after birth. At birth, the neonate's brain weighs only 25 percent of that of an adult brain. By the end of the second year, the brain weighs about 80 percent; by puberty, it weighs nearly 100 percent of that of an adult brain.

Reflexes and motor skills

Because infants cannot endure on their own, newborns have specific built-in or prewired abilities for survival and adaptive purposes. **Reflexes** are automatic reactions to stimulation that enable infants to respond to the environment before any learning has taken place. For instance, babies automatically suck when presented with a nipple, turn their heads when a parent speaks, grasp at a finger that is pressed into their hand, and startle when exposed to loud noises. Some reflexes, such as blinking, are permanent. Others, such as grasping, disappear after several months and eventually become voluntary responses. Common infant motor reflexes appear in Table 4-1.

Table 4-1: Common Infant Motor Reflexes

Reflex	*Stimulus/Action*
Blinking	In response to a puff of air, the infant closes both eyes.
Babinski	In response to stroking the side of its foot, the infant twists its foot inward and fans out its toes.
Grasping	In response to an object pressed against its palm, the infant attempts to grasp the object.
Moro	In response to a shock or loud noise, the infant arches its back and throws its arms outward.

Reflex	Stimulus/Action
Rooting	In response to stroking its cheek, the infant turns its head toward the touch and attempts to suck.
Stepping	In response to holding the infant so that its feet barely touch a surface, the infant "walks."
Sucking	In response to inserting a finger or nipple into its mouth, the infant begins rhythmically sucking.
Babkin	In response to stroking its forehead, the infant turns its head and opens its mouth.
Plantar	In response to touching the ball of the foot, the infant curls its toes under.

Motor skills, or behavioral abilities, develop in conjunction with physical growth. In other words, infants must learn to engage in motor activities within the context of their changing bodies. At about 1 month, infants may lift their chins while lying flat on their stomachs. Within another month, infants may raise their chests from the same position. By the fourth month, infants may grasp rattles, as well as sit with support. By the fifth month, infants may roll over, and by the eighth month, infants may be able to sit without assistance. At about 10 months, toddlers may stand while holding onto an object for support. At about 14 months, toddlers may stand alone and perhaps even walk. Of course, these ages for each motor-skill milestone are averages; the rates of physical and motor developments differ among children depending on a variety of factors, including heredity, the amount of activity the child participates in, and the amount of attention the child receives.

Motor development follows **cephalocaudal** (center and upper body) and **proximodistal** (extremities and lower body) patterns, so that motor skills become refined first from the center and upper body and later from the extremities and lower body. For example, swallowing is refined before walking, and arm movements are refined before hand movements.

Sensation and perception

Normal infants are capable of **sensation,** or the ability to respond to sensory information in the external world. These infants are born with functioning **sensory organs,** specialized structures of the body containing sensory receptors, which receive stimuli from the environment. **Sensory receptors** convert environmental energy into nervous system signals that the brain can understand and interpret. For example, the sensory receptors can convert light waves into visual images. The human senses include seeing, hearing, smelling, touching, and tasting.

Newborns are very nearsighted, but visual **acuity,** or ability, develops quickly. Although infant vision is not as good as adult vision, babies may respond visually to their surroundings from birth. Infants are particularly attracted to objects of light-and-dark contrasts, such as the human face. Depth perception also comes within a few months. Newborns may also respond to tastes, smells, and sounds, especially the sound of the human voice. In fact, newborns may almost immediately distinguish between the primary caregiver and others on the basis of sight, sound, and smell. Infant sensory abilities improve considerably during the first year.

Perception is the psychological process by which the human brain processes the sensory data collected by the sensory organs. Visually, infants are aware of **depth** (the relationship between foreground and background) and **size and shape constancy** (the consistent size and shape of objects). This latter ability is necessary for infants to learn about events and objects.

Learning

Learning is the process that results in relatively permanent change in behavior based on experience. Infants learn in a variety of ways. In **classical conditioning (Pavlovian),** learning occurs by association when a stimulus that evokes a certain response becomes associated with a different stimulus that originally did not cause that response. After the two stimuli associate in the subject's brain, the new stimulus then elicits the same response as the original. For instance, in psychologist John B. Watson's experiments with 11-month-old "Little Albert" in the 1920s, Watson classically conditioned Albert to fear a small white rat by pairing *the sight of* the rat with a loud, frightening noise. The once-neutral white rat then became a feared stimulus through associative learning. Babies younger than age 3 months generally do not learn well through classical conditioning.

In **operant conditioning (Skinnerian),** learning occurs through the application of rewards and/or punishments. Reinforcements increase behaviors, while punishments decrease behaviors. **Positive reinforcements** are pleasant stimuli that are added to increase behavior; **negative reinforcements** are unpleasant stimuli that are removed to increase behavior. Because reinforcements always increase behavior, negative reinforcement is not the same as punishment. For example, a parent who spanks a child to make him stop misbehaving is using punishment, while a parent who takes away a child's privileges to make him study harder is using negative reinforcement. **Shaping** is the gradual application of operant conditioning. For example, an infant who learns that smiling elicits positive parental attention will smile at its parents more. Babies generally respond well to operant conditioning.

In **observational learning,** learning is achieved by observing and imitating others, as in the case of an infant who learns to clap by watching and imitating an older sibling. This form of learning is perhaps the fastest and most natural means by which infants and toddlers acquire new skills.

Health

Normal functioning of the newborn's various body systems is vital to its short-term and long-term health. Less than 1 percent of babies experience **birth trauma,** or injury incurred during birth. Longitudinal studies have shown that birth trauma, low birth weight, and early sickness can affect later physical and mental health but usually only if these children grow up in impoverished environments. Most babies tend to be rather hardy and are able to compensate for less-than-ideal situations early in life.

Nevertheless, some children are born with or are exposed to conditions that pose greater challenges. For example, **phenylketonuria (PKU)** is an inherited metabolic disorder in which a child lacks phenylalanine hydroxylase, the enzyme necessary to eliminate excess **phynelalanine,** an essential amino acid, from the body. Failure to feed a special diet to a child with PKU in the first 3 to 6 weeks of life will result in mentally retardation. Currently, all 50 states require PKU screening for newborns.

Poor nutrition, hygiene, and medical care also expose a child to unnecessary health risks. Parents need to ensure that their infant eats well, is clean, and receives adequate medical attention. For instance, proper immunization is critical in preventing such contagious diseases as diptheria, measles, mumps, Rubella, and polio. A licensed health-care specialist can provide parents with charts detailing recommended childhood immunizations.

Infant mortality refers to the percentage of babies that die within the first year of life. In the United States today, about 9 babies out of every 1,000 live births die within the first year — a significantly smaller percentage than was reported only 50 years ago. This decrease in infant mortality is due to improvements in prenatal care and medicine in general. However, minority infants tend to be at a higher risk of dying, as are low birthweight, premature, and postmature babies. The leading causes of infant death are congenital birth defects, such as heart valve problems or pregnancy complications, and **sudden infant death syndrome (SIDS).**

SIDS is the unexpected and unexplained death of an apparently healthy infant. Postmortem autopsies of the SIDS infant usually provide no clues as to the cause of death. As far as authorities know, choking, vomiting, or suffocating does not cause SIDS. Two suspected causes include infant brain dysfunction and parental smoking, both prenatally and postnatally. In the United States, between 1 and 2 out of every 1,000 infants under age 1 die of SIDS each year.

Cognitive Development in Infancy and Toddlerhood

Much of modern cognitive developmental theory stems from the work of the Swiss psychologist, Jean Piaget. In the 1920s, Piaget observed that children's reasoning and understanding capabilities differed depending on their age. Piaget proposed that all children progress through a series of cognitive stages of development, just as they progress through a series of physical stages of development. According to Piaget, the rate at which children pass through these cognitive stages may vary, but boys and girls eventually pass through all the stages, in the same order.

Piaget's sensorimotor stage

During Piaget's **sensorimotor stage** (birth to age 2), infants and toddlers learn by doing: looking, hearing, touching, grasping, and sucking. The learning process appears to begin with coordinating movements of the body with incoming sensory data. As infants intentionally attempt to interact with the environment, infants learn that certain actions lead to specific consequences. These experiences are the beginning of the infants' understanding of cause-and-effect relationships.

Piaget divided the sensorimotor stage into six substages. In stage 1 (birth through month 1), infants exclusively use their reflexes, and their cognitive capabilities are limited. In stage 2 (months 1 through 4), infants engage in behaviors that accidentally produce specific effects.

Infants then repeat the behavior to obtain the same effect. An example is the infant's learning to suck on a pacifier following a series of trial-and-error attempts to use the new object. In stage 3 (months 4 through 8), infants begin to explore the impact of their behaviors on the environment. In stage 4 (months 8 through 12), infants purposefully carry out goal-directed behaviors.

Object permanence, or the knowledge that out-of-sight objects still exist, may begin to appear at about month 9 as infants search for objects that are hidden from view. In stage 5 (months 12 through 18), toddlers explore cause-and-effect relationships by intentionally manipulating causes to produce novel effects. For example, a toddler may attempt to make her parents smile by waving her hands at them. In stage 6 (months 18 through 24), toddlers begin to exhibit **representational** (symbolic) thought, demonstrating that they have started to internalize symbols as objects, such as people, places, and things. The child at this stage, for instance, uses words to refer to specific items, such as milk, dog, papa, or mama.

Other Piagetian concepts

Piaget's model introduces several other important concepts. Piaget termed the infant's innate thinking processes as **schemas.** In the sensorimotor period, these mental processes coordinate sensory, perceptual, and motor information so that infants eventually develop mental representations. In other words, reflexes provide the basis for schemas, which in turn provide the basis for representational thinking. For example, a child repeatedly touches and sees its rattle and thus learns to identify the rattle by forming an internalized image of it.

According to Piaget, cognitive development occurs from two processes: adaptation and equilibrium.

Adaptation involves children changing their behavior to meet situational demands and consists of two subprocesses: assimilation and accommodation.

- **Assimilation** is the application of previous concepts to new concepts, such as a child who refers to a whale as a fish.

- **Accommodation** is the altering of previous concepts in the face of new information, such as a child who discovers that some creatures living in the ocean are not fish and then correctly refers to a whale as a mammal.

Equilibrium is Piaget's term for the basic process underlying the human ability to adapt—is the search for balance between self and the world. Equilibrium involves the matching of children's adaptive functioning to situational demands, such as when a child realizes that he is one member of a family and not the center of the world. Equilibrium, which helps remove inconsistencies between reality and personal perspectives, keeps children moving along the developmental pathway, allowing them to make increasingly effective adaptations and decisions.

Evaluating Piagetian theory

The majority of researchers today accept Piaget's primary tenet: New cognitive skills build upon previous cognitive skills. Researchers see infants and toddlers as active learners who purposefully see, touch, and do, and who consequently develop additional cognitive skills. Developmentalists see cognitive development as involving both advancement and limitation. Devlopmentalists also applaud Piaget's role in stimulating professional interest in the cognitive world of children.

Piaget's research and theories are not unchallenged, however. Some of the more prominent critics of Piaget include Robbie Case, Pierr Dasen, Kurt Fischer, and Elizabeth Spelke. These critics and others maintain that the stages of development described by Piaget are not so distinct and clearly defined as Piaget originally indicated. These detractors also note that all children do not necessarily pass through Piaget's stages in precisely the same way or order. Piaget was aware of this phenomenon, which he termed **decalage,** but he never adequately explained decalage in light of the rest of his model.

Critics also suggest that toddlers and preschoolers are not as egocentric or as easily deceived as Piaget believed. Preschoolers may empathize with others, or put themselves into another person's shoes, and young children may make inferences and use logic. Preschoolers also develop cognitive abilities in relation to particular social and cultural contexts. These abilities may develop differently within enriched or deprived cultural environments. In other words, children who grow up in middle and upper-class families may have more opportunities to develop cognitive skills than those who grow up in lower-class families.

Children appear to employ and more deeply understand symbols at an earlier age than was previously thought. In as early as the first 3 months, infants display a basic understanding of how the world works. For example, infants pay closer attention to objects that seem to defy physical laws, such as balls that appear to roll through walls or rattles that appear to hang in mid-air as opposed to stationary objects.

Memory
Central to early cognitive development is memory development. **Memory** is the ability to encode, retain, and recall information over time. Researchers generally refer to **sensory** (less than 1 second), **short-term** (less than 30 seconds), and **long-term** (indefinite) memory stores. Children are not able to habituate or learn if they are unable to encode objects, people, and places and eventually recall them from long-term memory.

Researchers are unclear about the exact nature of infantile memory, however. The unclear facts about infantile memory include how long such memories last, as well as how easily memories are retrieved from long-term stores. Evidence suggests that babies begin forming long-term memories during the first 6 months. Infants may recognize and remember primary caretakers, as well as familiar surroundings. Early memory experiences help infants and toddlers to understand basic concepts and categories, all of which are central to more completely understanding the world around them.

Language

Language skills begin to emerge during the first 2 years. **Psycholinguists,** specialists in the study of language, indicate that language is an outgrowth of children's ability to use symbols. Physical development determines the timing of language development. As the brains develop, preschoolers acquire the capacity for representational thinking, which lays the foundation for language. In this way, cognitive development also determines the timing of language development. **Observational learning** (imitation) and **operant conditioning** (reinforcement) play important roles in the early acquisition of language. Children are reinforced to speak meaningfully and reasonably by imitating the language of their caregivers; in turn caregivers are prompted to respond meaningfully and reasonably to the children.

Psycholinguists are especially interested in three elements of language: **content** (what is meant), **form** (what is actually said), and **use** (how and to whom it is said). Psycholinguists claim that all members of the human race use these three elements in some combination to communicate with each other. Noam Chomsky suggested that the learning of a language is rooted in an inborn capacity to comprehend and structure language, which he defined as the language acquisition device.

According to psycholinguists, acquisition of language also occurs within a social and cultural context. Socializing agents—family members, peers, teachers, and the media—teach children how to think and act in socially acceptable ways. Children learn about the world and society as they learn to use language.

Infants and toddlers understand language before actually speaking language; children have **receptive language,** or an understanding of the spoken and written word, before acquiring **productive language,** or an ability to use the spoken or written word. Before saying their first words, infants babble. That is, babies make meaningless sounds while learning to control their vocalizations. By the end of the first year, most babies are uttering single words. Soon infants begin to use **holophrastic speech,** or single words that convey complete ideas. "Mama" (meaning

"Mama, come here!") and "Milk!" (meaning "Give me some milk!") are examples of holophrastic speech. When starting to put words together to form sentences, children first use **telegraphic speech,** in which words that are the most meaningful are used, such as "Want milk!"

During **infancy** and **toddlerhood,** children easily attach to others. Youngsters normally form their initial primary relationships with their parents and other family members. Because infants are utterly dependent on caregivers for food, clothing, warmth, and nurturing, Erik Erikson determined that children's primary task during this first **psychosocial** stage of life is to learn to trust their caregivers. As they form relationships and develop an organized sense of self, children's first few years set the stage for both immediate and later psychosocial development, including the emergence of **prosocial behavior,** or the capacity to help, cooperate, and share with others.

Personality Development in Infancy and Toddlerhood

Personality includes those stable psychological characteristics that make each human being unique. Both children and adults evidence personality **traits** (long-term characteristics, such as temperament) and **states** (changeable characteristics, such as moodiness). While considerable debate continues over the origin and development of personality, most experts agree that personality traits and states form early in life. A combination of hereditary, psychological, and social influences is most likely responsible for the formation of personality.

Infants are typically **egocentric,** or self-centered, and are primarily concerned with satisfying physical desires, such as hunger. Sigmund Freud viewed this focus on physical gratification as a form of self-pleasuring. Because infants are particularly interested in activities involving the mouth (sucking and biting, for example), Freud labeled the first year of life as the **oral stage** of psychosexual development.

According to Freud too little or too much stimulation of a particular **erogenous zone** (sensitive area of the body) at a particular psychosexual stage of development leads to **fixation** (literally, being stuck) at that stage. Multiple fixations are possible at multiple stages. In the case of infants, fixation at the oral stage gives rise to adult personality traits centered on the mouth. Adult oral-focused habits may take the form of overeating, drinking, and smoking. Adults are especially prone to regressing to such childhood fixation behaviors during times of stress and upset.

Theorists, after Freud, have offered additional perspectives on infant personality development. Perhaps the most important of these developments is Melanie Klein's **object-relations theory.** According to Klein, the inner core of personality stems from the early relationship with the mother. While Freud speculated that the child's fear of a powerful father determines personality, Klein theorized that the child's need for a powerful mother is more important. In other words, the child's fundamental human drive is to be in relationships with others, and the first relationship the child establishes is usually with the mother.

Why the phrase "object-relations"? Why did Klein use the word "object" rather than "human"? Following intensive observation and the study of many children, Klein surmised that the infant bonds to an object rather than a person, because the infant is unable to understand fully what a person is. The infant's limited perspective may process only an evolving perception of what a person is.

In this object-relations theory, the infant interacts with the mother, mostly during times of eye contact and breast-feeding. The infant then internalizes an image of the mother—good or bad—that may or may not be representative of how the mother truly is. Eventually, during a complex psychological process of adjusting to loss and separation, the child learns to distinguish between self and object at a very basic level. If all goes well, the psychologically healthy child is then able to separate good and bad, and self and object. If all does not go well, the child is then unable to accept the good and bad sides of the self and of the mother; the child may be unable to separate the concept of a bad mother from a good self.

In object-relations theory, girls are better adjusted psychosocially than boys. Girls become extensions of their mothers; as a result, girls do not need to separate from their mothers. Boys, on the other, must separate from their mothers to become independent. This perspective is in contrast to Freudian theory, in which boys develop a stronger **superego** (conscience) than girls, because boys have penises and girls do not. According to Freud, his superego theory supported why boys more easily resolve their **Oedipal conflict** (a male's childhood sexual interest in his mother with accompanying aggression toward his father) than girls do their **Electra conflict** (a female's childhood sexual interest in her father with accompanying aggression toward her mother).

Some psychologists theorize that errors in early bonding and separating experiences may be responsible for later psychological problems. These problems include **borderline personality disorder,** which is characterized by rapid shifts in the liking and hating of self and others.

Family Relationships in Infancy and Toddlerhood

The baby's first relationship is generally with family members, to whom the infant expresses a range of emotions (and vice versa). If the social and emotional bonding between infant and family is faulty in some way, the child may never develop the trust, self-control, or emotional reasoning necessary to function effectively in the world. The quality of the relationship between child and parents—especially when the child is between the ages of 6 and 18 months—seems to determine the quality of the child's later relationships.

If physical contact between infant and parents is so vital to the emotional health of the infant, and important to the parents as well, most experts recommend that physical contact occur as soon after delivery as possible. Babies who are the recipients of immediate maternal contact seem to cry less and are happier and more secure than babies who do not receive immediate maternal contact. Fortunately, babies who are separated from their parents at birth are not necessarily doomed to a life of mental disorders. Immediate bonding is optimal, but infants and parents may later make up for an initial separation.

Attachment

Attachment is the process whereby one individual seeks nearness to another individual. In parent-child interactions, attachment is generally mutual and reciprocal. The infant looks and smiles at the parents, who look and smile at the infant. Indeed, communication between child and parents is basic at this level, but it is also profound. Psychologist John Bowlby suggests that infants are born preprogrammed for certain behaviors that guarantee bonding with their caregivers. Infants' crying, clinging, smiling, and cooing are designed to prompt parental feeding, holding, cuddling, and vocalizing. Parents may help instill trust in their infants as their infant children form attachments. Eye contact, touching, and timely feedings are perhaps the most important ways. These actions, of course, are also expressions of the love and affection parents have for their children.

Attachment is central to human existence, but so are separation and loss. Ultimately, relationships are eventually interrupted or dissolved on their own. Children must learn that nothing human is permanent, although learning this concept is not easy. Children between 7 and 24 months of age experience **separation anxiety,** or distress at the prospect of being left alone in an unfamiliar place. Related to separation anxiety is **stranger anxiety,** or distress in the presence of unfamiliar people. Separation and stranger anxieties are strong indicators of the attachment process, as the child may now distinguish between familiar and unfamiliar stimuli. Children without **multiple attachments** (lacking relationships with people other than the primary caregivers) seem more likely to develop separation and stranger anxieties.

According to Bowlby, children who are separated from their parents progress through three stages: protest, despair, and detachment. After first refusing to accept the separation, and then losing hope, the child finally accepts the separation and begins to respond to the attention of new caregivers.

Social deprivation, or the absence of attachment, has profoundly negative effects on children. For instance, children who have been institutionalized without close or continuous attachments for long periods of time display pathological levels of depression, withdrawal, apathy, and anxiety.

Parenting

Cultural and community standards, the social environment, and their children's behaviors determine parents' child-raising practices. Hence, different parents have different ideas regarding the raising of their children; the differences are seen in their communication methods or even in their decisions about the placement of their children in daycare.

Responding to an infant's needs through playing, vocalizing, feeding, and touching is certainly important to the child's psychosocial development. In fact, children who display strong attachments tend to have highly responsive mothers. But this important display of strong attachments does not always mean that caregivers should respond to everything infants do. Children must learn that all needs cannot be completely met all the time. The majority of caregivers respond to their infants most of, but not 100 percent of, the time. Problems seem to arise only when primary caregivers respond to infants less than 25 percent of the time. The children of nonresponsive mothers tend to be insecurely attached, which may simultaneously lead to overdependence upon and rejection of authority figures later in adulthood.

Strong communication between parents and children leads to strong attachments and relationships. **Mutuality,** or synchronous (back and forth) interaction, particularly during the first few months, predicts a secure relationship between parents and infants. Mutual behaviors include taking turns approaching and withdrawing, looking and touching, and "talking" with each other. However, infants may resist mutuality when overstimulated. Resistant behaviors in such instances include turning away, closing the eyes, wiggling, and crying. In the second year, mutual behaviors such as taking turns, give-and-take, and imitating predict later prosocial behaviors. Soon afterward, children learn more complex rules of social interactions—how to invite others to play games, how to follow rules, how to cooperate, and how to share toys.

Because the first few months and years of life are so critical to children's future psychosocial development, some parents worry about having to place their infants and toddlers in daycares and preschools. Research suggests, however, that children who attend daycares are not at a disadvantage regarding development of self, prosocial behavior, or cognitive functioning. In fact, daycares and preschools offer children enriched social environments, with structured opportunities to interact with diverse groups of youngsters. Many authorities argue that daycare placement, coupled with quality time with the parents whenever possible, provides for better and earlier socialization than may otherwise occur.

Sexuality in Infancy and Toddlerhood

The word **sexuality** conjures up many diverse images, but childhood sexuality is rarely among these images. When pondering the sexuality of youth, adults invariably think of teenagers and young adults. These thoughts are oftentimes in terms of negatives and social problems, including sexually transmitted diseases and teenage pregnancy. Many Americans do not acknowledge the sexual nature of infants and toddlers. Rather than accepting children as sexual beings in process, they categorize them as **asexual,** or not having sexual interests or abilities. The misconceptions of most Americans do little to create an accurate picture of human sexuality in general. As scientists, philosophers, and other experts have established, human sexuality is an essential aspect of human experience at all ages. Human sexuality is a lifelong process that begins at birth and ends with death.

With respect to infants specifically, physical contact between infant and parents is a source of pleasure. Maternal contact coupled with the infant's biting and sucking seems to stimulate pleasurable reflexes. Babies are actually sexual in the sense of physical responsiveness. Female babies produce vaginal lubrication, and male babies have penile erections. Ultrasounds have even shown developing male fetuses with erections months before birth. But infants are not aware of their sexual experiences as sources of eroticism. Infants are unaware of the sexual significance of their relationship with the parents, but babies are aware of pleasurable sensations associated with physical contact with the parents. As infants acquire **motor skills** (the ability to move with intention) and begin to explore their own bodies, babies learn to handle their genitals. This deliberate genital touching quickly becomes associated with pleasure.

Co-sleeping

A common concern among family members is the issue of **co-sleeping,** or children sleeping in the same bed as their parents. Does co-sleeping lead to blurred sexual boundaries? Are children who sleep in the same bed as their parents more prone to later emotional problems than those children who do not? Does co-sleeping lead to a higher occurrence of sexual abuse of children? While classical Freudians have traditionally argued against co-sleeping on the grounds that it interferes with the resolution of the Oedipal and Electra conflicts, the answer to all these questions seems to be *no.* Current research indicates that children who co-sleep with their parents are just as physically and emotionally healthy as those who do not. The age at which children stop sleeping with their parents is not predetermined; the age depends on when the parents believe the right time has come.

Gender Development

Gender refers to an individual's anatomical sex, or **sexual assignment,** and the cultural and social aspects of being male or female. An individual's personal sense of maleness or femaleness is his or her **gender identity.** Outward expression of gender identity, according to cultural and social expectations, is a **gender role.** Either gender may live out a gender role (a man or a woman, for instance, can be a home-maker) but not a **sex role,** which is anatomically limited to one gender (only a woman can gestate and give birth).

Gender identity

Gender identity appears to form very early in life and is most likely irreversible by age 4. Although the exact cause of gender identity remains unknown, biological, psychological, and social variables clearly influence the process. Genetics, prenatal and postnatal hormones, differences in the brain and the reproductive organs, and socialization all interact to mold a toddler's gender identity. The differences brought about by physiological processes ultimately interact with social-learning influences to establish clear gender identity.

Psychological and social influences on gender identity

Gender identity is ultimately derived from chromosomal makeup and physical appearance, but this derivation of gender identity does not mean that psychosocial influences are missing. **Gender socialization,** or the process whereby a child learns the norms and roles that society has created for his or her gender, plays a significant role in the establishment of her or his sense of femaleness or maleness. If a child learns she is a female and is raised as a female, the child believes she is a female; if a child is told he is a male and is raised as a male, the child believes he is male.

Beginning at birth, most parents treat their children according to the appearance of their genitals. Parents even handle their baby girls less aggressively than their baby boys. Children quickly develop a clear understanding that they are either female or male, as well as a strong desire to adopt gender-appropriate mannerisms and behaviors. This understanding normally occurs within 2 years of age, according to many authorities. In short, biology sets the stage, but children's interactions with social environments actually determine the nature of gender identity.

Gender roles

Gender roles are both cultural and personal. These roles determine how males and females think, speak, dress, and interact within the context of society. Learning plays a role in this process of shaping gender roles. These **gender schemas** are deeply embedded cognitive frameworks regarding what defines masculine and feminine. While various **socializing agents**—educators, peers, movies, television, music, books, and religion—teach and reinforce gender roles throughout a child's life span, parents probably exert the greatest influence, especially when their children are very young.

Developmentalists indicate that adults perceive and treat female and male infants differently. Parents probably do this in response to having been recipients of gender expectations as young children themselves. Traditionally, fathers teach boys how to fix and build things; mothers teach girls how to cook, sew, and keep house. Children then receive parental approval when they conform to gender expectations and adopt culturally accepted and conventional roles. All of these lessons are reinforced by additional socializing agents, such as the media. In other words, learning gender roles always occurs within a social context, with the values of the parents and society being passed along to the children of successive generations.

Ages 2 through 6 are the **early childhood** years, or preschool years. Like infants and toddlers, preschoolers grow quickly—both physically and cognitively. A short chubby toddler who can barely talk suddenly becomes a taller, leaner child who talks incessantly. Especially evident during early childhood is the fact that development is truly **integrated:** The biological, psychological, and social changes occurring at this time (as well as throughout the rest of the life span) are interrelated.

Physical Development in Early Childhood

Although physical development in preschoolers is dramatic, the development is slower and more stable than during infancy. Some important influences on physical development during the preschool period include changes in the child's brain, gross and fine motor skills, and health.

Physical changes

Children begin to lose their baby fat, or chubbiness, around age 3. Toddlers soon acquire the leaner, more athletic look associated with childhood. The child's trunk and limbs grow longer, and the abdominal muscles form, tightening the appearance of the stomach. Even at this early stage of life, boys tend to have more muscle mass than girls. The preschoolers' physical proportions also continue to change, with their heads still being disproportionately large, but less so than in toddlerhood.

Three-year-old preschoolers may grow to be about 38 inches tall and weigh about 32 pounds. For the next 3 years, healthy preschoolers grow an additional 2 to 3 inches and gain from 4 to 6 pounds per year.

By age 6, children reach a height of about 46 inches and weigh about 46 pounds. Of course, these figures are averages and differ from child to child, depending on socioeconomic status, nourishment, health, and heredity factors.

Brain development

Brain and nervous system developments during early childhood also continue to be dramatic. The better developed the brain and nervous systems are, the more complex behavioral and cognitive abilities children are capable of.

The brain is comprised of two halves, the right and left **cerebral hemispheres. Lateralization** refers to the localization of assorted functions, competencies, and skills in either or both hemispheres. Specifically, language, writing, logic, and mathematical skills seem to be located in the left hemisphere, while creativity, fantasy, artistic, and musical skills seem to be located in the right hemisphere. Although the hemispheres may have separate functions, these brain masses almost always coordinate their functions and work together.

The two cerebral hemispheres develop at different rates, with the left hemisphere developing more fully in early childhood (ages 2 to 6), and the right hemisphere developing more fully in middle childhood (ages 7 to 11). The left hemisphere predominates earlier and longer, which may explain why children acquire language so early and quickly.

Another aspect of brain development is **handedness,** or preference for using one hand over the other. Handedness appears to be strongly established by middle childhood. About 90 percent of the general population is right-handed, while the rest of the population is left-handed and/or **ambidextrous.** A person is ambidextrous if he or she shows no preference for one hand over the other. Typically, right-handedness is associated with left-cerebral dominance and left-handedness with right-cerebral dominance.

The nervous system undergoes changes in early childhood, too. The majority of a child's **neurons,** or cells that make up nerves, form prenatally. However, the **glial cells,** (nervous system support cells surrounding neurons) that nourish, insulate, and remove waste from the neurons without actually transmitting information themselves, develop most rapidly during infancy, toddlerhood, and early childhood. The **myelin sheaths** that surround, insulate, and increase the efficiency of neurons (by speeding up the action potential along the axon) also form rapidly during the first few years of life. The postnatal developments of glial cells and myelin sheaths help to explain why older children may perform behaviors that younger children are not capable of.

Motor skills

Motor skills are physical abilities or capacities. **Gross motor skills,** which include running, jumping, hopping, turning, skipping, throwing, balancing, and dancing, involve the use of large bodily movements. **Fine motor skills,** which include drawing, writing, and tying shoelaces, involve the use of small bodily movements. Both gross and fine motor skills develop and are refined during early childhood; however, fine motor skills develop more slowly in preschoolers. If you compare the running abilities of a 2-year-old and a 6-year-old, for example, you may notice the limited running skills of the 2-year-old. But the differences are even more striking when comparing a 2-year-old and 6-year-old who are tying shoelaces. The 2-year-old has difficulty grasping the concept before ever attempting or completing the task.

Albert Bandura's theory of **observational learning** is applicable to preschoolers' learning gross and fine motor skills. Bandura states that once children are biologically capable of learning certain behaviors, children must do the following in order to develop new skills:

1. Observe the behavior in others.

2. Form a mental image of the behavior.

3. Imitate the behavior.

4. Practice the behavior.

5. Be motivated to repeat the behavior.

In other words, children must be ready, have adequate opportunities, and be interested in developing motor skills to become competent at those skills.

Health

Preschoolers are generally quite healthy, but may develop medical problems. Typical minor illnesses, which usually last no more than 14 days, include colds, coughs, and stomachaches. Respiratory ailments are the most common illnesses among children at this age because preschoolers' lungs have not yet fully developed. Most childhood illnesses usually do not require a physician's or nurse's attention. Additionally, minor illnesses may help children to learn coping skills, particularly how to deal with physical discomfort and distress. Minor illnesses may also help children learn **empathy,** or how to understand someone else's discomfort and distress.

In contrast, major illnesses of early childhood, which are severe and last longer than 14 days, include influenza, pneumonia, cancer, and human immunodeficiency virus (HIV) and acquired immunodeficiency syndrome (AIDS). AIDS is among the top 10 causes of death for small children, and to date, more than 25,000 children in the United States have died from AIDS and related complications. Besides physical problems, children suffering from long-term illnesses have significant psychological hurdles to overcome, including developmental delays, anxiety, and pain. Moreover, children afflicted by AIDS may also have parents with AIDS and must learn to cope with household stress, depression, and the potential loss of their caregivers.

Certain children experience more illnesses than their peers. Poverty, family stress, being in daycare, or being from a large family (more family members increase the risk that someone may get sick and pass along the illness to other family members) is correlated with increased risk of illness in the preschooler age group.

The majority of deaths during early childhood are due to accidental injuries rather than illnesses. The most common source of deadly accidents for preschoolers is the automobile. Other causes of childhood death include drowning, suffocating, being burned, being poisoned, and falling from heights. Young children's sense of adventure often outweighs their understanding of the dangers inherent in various activities and situations. Therefore, adequate adult supervision is necessary at all times whether at home, in daycare, or on the playground.

Cognitive Development in Early Childhood

Preschoolers provide remarkable examples of how children play an active role in their own cognitive development, especially in their attempts to understand, explain, organize, manipulate, construct, and predict. Young children also see patterns in objects and events of the world and then attempt to organize those patterns to explain the world.

At the same time, preschoolers have cognitive limitations. Children have trouble controlling their own attention and memory functions, confuse superficial appearances with reality, and focus on a single aspect of an experience at a time. Across cultures, young children tend to make these same kinds of immature cognitive errors.

Piaget referred to the cognitive development occurring between ages 2 and 7 as the **preoperational stage.** In this stage, children increase their use of language and other symbols, their imitation of adult behaviors, and their play. Young children develop a fascination with words—both good and bad language. Children also play games of make-believe: using an empty box as a car, playing family with siblings, and nurturing imaginary friendships.

Piaget also described the preoperational stage in terms of what children cannot do. Piaget used the term **operational** to refer to reversible abilities that children had not yet developed. By reversible, Piaget referred to mental or physical actions that can go back and forth—meaning that they can occur in more than one way, or direction. Adding (3 + 3 = 6) and subtracting (6 − 3 = 3) are examples of reversible actions. Children at this stage, according to Piaget, make use of magical thinking based on their own sensory and perceptual abilities and are easily misled. Children engage in magical thinking, for instance, while speaking with their parents on the telephone and then asking for a gift, expecting it to arrive via the telephone.

Piaget believed that preschoolers' cognitive abilities are limited by **egocentrism**—the inability to distinguish between their own point of view and the point of view of others. The capacity to be egocentric is apparent at all stages of cognitive development, but egocentricity is particularly evident during the preschool years. Young children eventually overcome this early form of egocentrism when learning that others have differing views, feelings, and desires. Then children may interpret others' motives and use those interpretations to communicate mutually—and therefore more effectively—with others. Preschoolers eventually learn to adjust their vocal pitches, tones, and speeds to match those of the listener. Because mutual communication requires effort and preschoolers are still egocentric, children may lapse into egocentric (nonmutual) speech during times of frustration. In other words, children (and adults) may regress to earlier behavioral patterns when their cognitive resources are stressed and overwhelmed.

Piaget indicated that young children have not mastered **classification,** or the ability to group according to features. Neither have they mastered **serial ordering,** or the ability to group according to logical progression. While possibly inherent in young children, these abilities are not fully realized until later.

Piaget also believed that young children cannot comprehend **conservation,** or the concept that physical properties remain constant even as appearance and form change. Young children have trouble understanding that the same amount of liquid poured into containers of different shapes remains the same. A preoperational child will tell you that a handful of pennies is more money than a single five-dollar bill. According to Piaget, when children develop the cognitive capacity to conserve (around age 7), children move into the next stage of development, concrete operations (described in Chapter 8).

As noted in Chapter 4, current research implies that children are not as suggestible, operational, magical, or egocentric as Piaget surmised. In studying children's use of symbols and representational thinking, for example, researcher Renee Baillargeon found that preschoolers as young as 2½ are able to employ reversible mental thinking. Baillargeon's research involved the following experiment: Two objects—a large red pillow and a miniature red pillow—are hidden in a large room and a miniature replica of the room, respectively; shown where the miniature pillow is hiding in the miniature room, a child locates the corresponding large pillow in the large room. Baillargeon suggested that such abilities are indicative of symbolic thought, in which objects represent not only themselves but also other objects as well.

In contrast to Piaget's theories of childhood egocentrism, similar studies indicate that children can and do relate to the frame of reference of others. Two- and three-year-olds, for instance, have been shown to modify their speech in an effort to communicate more clearly with younger children. Researcher John Flavell suggested that preschoolers progress through two stages of **empathy,** or sharing perspectives. At the first level, around ages 2 through 3, the child understands that others have their own experiences. At the second level, around ages 4 through 5, the child interprets others' experiences, including their thoughts and feelings. This shifting in perspective is indicative of cognitive changes: At the first level, the child focuses on appearances; at the second level, on reality as they understand it. Hence, young children develop **social cognition,** or an understanding of their social world, however immature that understanding may be.

Typical 5-year-olds are interested in how their minds and the minds of others work. Children eventually form a **theory of mind,** an awareness and understanding of others' states of mind and accompanying actions. Children can then predict how others will think and react, particularly based on their own experiences in the world.

Current research of 2- to 5-year-olds clearly demonstrates that Piaget incorrectly assumed that preoperational children are only literally minded. In fact, these children can think logically, project themselves into others' situations, and interpret their surroundings. So while the cognitive qualities of Piaget's preoperational stage may apply to some or even many children, these qualities do not apply to all children.

Memory

As defined in Chapter 4, **memory** is the ability to encode, retain, and recall information over time. Children must learn to encode objects, people, and places and later be able to recall them from long-term memory.

Young children do not remember as well as older children and adults. Furthermore, these children are better at recognition than at recall memory tasks. Researchers suspect several possible causes for this development. One explanation is that preschoolers may be lacking in certain aspects of brain development necessary for mature memory skills. Another explanation is that preschoolers do not have the same number and kinds of experiences to draw upon as adults when processing information. Another reason is that young children lack **selective attention,** meaning they are more easily distracted. Still another explanation is that children lack the same quality and quantity of effective mnemonic strategies as adults.

Preschoolers, nonetheless, demonstrate an intense interest in learning. What a child may lack in skills is made up for in initiative. Children have an inherent curiosity about the world, which prompts a need to learn as much as possible, as quickly as possible. Some young children may become frustrated when learning does not come about as quickly or remembering as efficiently as older children. When learning situations are structured so that children may succeed—setting reasonably attainable goals and providing guidance and support—children can be exceptionally mature in their ability to process information.

Language

Language skills also continue to improve during early childhood. As noted in Chapter 4, language is an outgrowth of a child's ability to use symbols. Thus, as their brains develop and acquire the capacity for representational thinking, children also acquire and refine language skills.

Some researchers, like Roger Brown, have measured language development by the average number of words in a child's sentences. The more words a child uses in sentences, the more sophisticated the child's language development. Brown suggested that language develops in sequential stages: utterances, phrases with inflections, simple sentences, and complex sentences. Basic syntax, according to Brown, is not fully realized until about age 10.

Preschoolers learn many new words. Parents, siblings, peers, teachers, and the media provide opportunities for preschoolers to increase their vocabulary. Consequently, the acquisition of language occurs within a social and cultural context. Socializing agents provide more than just words and their meanings, however. These agents teach children how to think and act in socially acceptable ways. Children learn about society as they learn about language. Society's values, norms, **folkways** (informal rules of acceptable behavior), and **mores** (formal rules of acceptable behavior) are transmitted by how parents and others demonstrate the use of words.

Around the world and in the United States, some young children are **bilingual,** or able to speak more than one language. These children learn two languages simultaneously, usually as a result of growing up with bilingual parents who speak both languages at home. Many of these bilingual children may fluently speak both languages by age 4.

Some ethnic children learn to speak a **dialect,** or variations of a language, before they learn to speak standard English. A debate rages today over whether or not ethnic dialects should be considered equal in value to conventional languages.

For example, some educators believe dialects such as Ebonics (Black English) and Spanglish (Spanish English) should be taught in American classrooms alongside traditional English. According to these educators, encouraging dialects improves a child's self-esteem, increases a child's chances of understanding classroom material, and celebrates multicultural diversity. Other educators, however, worry that Ebonics and Spanglish put children at risk of not mastering standard English, which in turn puts them at a disadvantage in preparing for college and the workforce.

The preschool years are associated with major developments in young children's socialization. No longer totally dependent on their parents, preschoolers begin the long road to becoming adept at functioning on their own in the world. During **early childhood** (ages 2–6), children gain some sense of being separate and independent from their parents. According to Erikson, the task of preschoolers is to develop **autonomy,** or **self-direction,** (ages 1–3), as well as **initiative,** or **enterprise** (ages 3–6).

Personality Development in Early Childhood

As defined in Chapter 5, **personality** includes those stable psychological characteristics that define each human being as unique. Both children and adults have personality **traits** (long-term characteristics, such as temperament) and **states** (changeable characteristics, such as moodiness). While a variety of explanations are possible, most experts agree that whatever the causes, an individual's personality is solidly established by the end of early childhood.

According to Freud, the second year of childhood is the **anal stage** of psychosexual development, when parents face many new challenges while toilet training their children. Fixations at this stage may give rise to characteristic personality traits that fully emerge in adulthood. These personality traits include **anal retention** (excessive neatness, organization, and withholding) or **anal expulsion** (messiness and altruism).

Personality theorists after Freud have attempted to explain early childhood personality development. Learning theorists claim that personality develops as a result of **classical conditioning** (Ivan Pavlov's learning by association), **operant conditioning** (B. F. Skinner's learning by reinforcement and punishment), and **observational learning** (Albert Bandura's learning by imitation). This latter category involves **identification,** or internalization, whereby children observe and adopt the values, ideas, and standards of their significant others. Cognitive psychologists speculate that personality arises, in part, from the attitudes and biases expressed by the adults around them. Gender theorists claim that personality develops from "gender identification" and "gender socialization" (see Chapter 5). Geneticists speculate that personality arises from "wired in" genetic and biochemical influences rather than psychosocial ones.

In the final analysis, no perspective alone can adequately explain the complex processes of personality development. A combination of psychosocial, parental, and biological influences are likely responsible for the ultimate determination of human traits and states.

Family Relationships in Early Childhood

Family relationships are critical to the physical, mental, and social health of growing preschoolers. Many aspects of the family—parenting techniques, discipline, the number and the birth order of siblings, the family's finances, the family's circumstances, the family's health, and more—contribute to young children's psychosocial development.

Parenting

Different parents employ different parenting techniques. The techniques parents choose depend on cultural and community standards, the situation, and the children's behavior at the time. The techniques that parents use to relate to their children are characterized by degrees of parental control and parental warmth. **Parental control** involves the degree to which parents are restrictive in their use of parenting techniques, and **parental warmth** involves the degree to which they are loving, affectionate, and approving in their use of these techniques. **Authoritarian parents** demonstrate high parental control and low parental warmth when parenting. **Permissive parents** demonstrate high parental warmth and low parental control when parenting. **Indifferent parents** demonstrate low parental control and low warmth. **Authoritative parents,** however, demonstrate appropriate levels of both parental control and warmth.

Parenting styles have a definite impact on children. The authoritative style of parenting fosters open communication and problem solving between parents and their children. In contrast, authoritarian parenting may produce fearful and dependent children. Permissive parenting may result in rebellious children. And indifferent parenting may render hostile and delinquent children. In two-parent families, in which each parent has a different parenting style, one parent's style often positively counterbalances the other parent's style. For instance, a woman's permissive style may counterbalance her husband's authoritarian style.

The willingness of parents to negotiate with their children in order to achieve common goals is highly desirable. This willingness does not imply, however, that everything within a family system is negotiable. Neither parents nor their children should be in charge all of the time; such a degree of control leads to unhealthy power struggles within the family. Parental negotiating teaches children that quality relationships can be **equitable,** or equal in terms of sharing rights, responsibilities, and decision making. Most negotiating home environments are warm, accommodating, and mutually supportive.

Siblings

Siblings are children's first and foremost peer group. Preschoolers may learn as much or more from their siblings as from their parents. Regardless of age differences, sibling relationships mirror other social relationships, providing basic preparation for dealing with people outside of the home. Only siblings may simultaneously have equal and unequal status in the home, and only siblings may provide opportunities (whether desired or not) for children to practice coping with the positives and negatives of human relationships.

Only children, or children without siblings, are not at a developmental disadvantage. Research confirms that onlies perform just as well as, if not better than, children with siblings on measures of personality, intelligence, and achievement. One explanation is that, like children who are first in the birth order, only children may have the undivided (or nearly undivided) attention of their parents, who in turn have more quality time to spend with their only children.

Family circumstances and social class

Without a doubt, family circumstances affect the development of young children, who tend to fare better in financially secure and intact households. Unfortunately, not all families have the resources to allow a parent to remain at home during the day or to purchase the best possible daycare services. In addition, not all families are able to access necessary health care. The long-term emotional consequences of coming from a family with a low socioeconomic status may be significant.

To see how far-reaching the effects of social class are on children's attitudes and development, sociologist Melvin Kohn studied differences in the parenting styles of working-class and middle-class parents. Kohn found that working-class parents tend to stress outward conformity in their children, while middle-class parents tend to stress self-expression, motivation, and curiosity in their children. Kohn concluded that social class—where the attitudes and behavior of parents are passed down to their children—also plays a role in young children's psychosocial development.

Friends and Playmates in Early Childhood

Early family attachments may determine the ease with which children form friendships and other relationships. Children who have loving, stable, and accepting relationships with their parents and siblings are generally more likely to form similar relationships with friends and playmates.

First friendships are created when a child is about age 3, although preschoolers may play together before that age. Much like adults, preschoolers tend to develop friendships with children who share common interests, are likable, offer support, and are similar in sizes and looks. Childhood friendships create opportunities for children to learn how to handle anger-provoking situations, to share, to learn values, and to practice more mature behaviors. Preschoolers who are popular with their peers excel at these activities. These children know how to be a friend, not just how to have friends. On the other hand, children who "tattle" or direct hostility toward their playmates tend to be less popular. In turn, aggressive children often have fewer friends, which fuels their hostility even more.

Sexuality in Early Childhood

Ages 3 to 6 mark the **phallic stage** of psychosexual development, when children experience heightened interest in their genitals. Freud speculated that near the end of the phallic stage, children are erotically attracted to the opposite-gender parent. In response to internal mental conflicts that arise because of this attraction, children identify with the same-gender parent at the resolution of the Oedipal Complex (boys) or Electra Complex (girls).

Most children masturbate at some point during the phallic stage. Parents may keep in mind that masturbation is widespread among children. No scientific evidence supports the position that masturbation is harmful in any way, with the exception of guilt and other negative emotions arising from others' reactions. Although parents may be shocked to learn that their children masturbate, vigorously prohibiting the practice may be psychologically damaging to the children over time. Instead, parents should help their children learn more about the socially appropriate use of their genitals.

Besides a growing interest in their own bodies, preschoolers become curious about the bodies of their siblings and playmates, especially boy-girl differences. That girls do not have a penis and boys do is of intense concern. This curiosity may lead to endless questions, as well as any of a number of peeking and doctor games, touching and exploration with peers, and watching one another urinate. Parents should understand that these normal activities are to be expected when done with same-age children and in moderation. Parents should also remain alert to the possibility of older siblings and children sexually exploiting younger children.

No evidence suggests that sexplay with same-gender children causes homosexuality, or that sexplay with peers leads to early sexual intercourse. Setting limits in nonpunitive and noncritical ways minimizes the possibility that the child will become confused, develop guilt, or later experience sexual problems.

Parents' expressions of affection influence their children's conceptions of love, because children's primary role models are their parents. How children eventually conceptualize and express love and affection is traceable back to their observations of their parents. And parents want to help their children become well-balanced, content, and fully functioning adults. Children's views of loving relationships and sex—positive or negative—are normally a reflection of the quality of love and affection expressed by the parents to each other and their children. Children who never witness love at home may find it impossible to feel or demonstrate love as adults.

Fear and Aggression in Early Childhood

Two negative emotions experienced during early childhood are **fear** (anxiety) and **aggression** (hostility).

Preschool children probably become fearful because of their remarkable fantasy life, and their inability to distinguish between reality and pretending. Childhood fears are usually temporary; these fears normally disappear with time. Preschoolers (ages 2–6) are typically afraid of animals, bodily injury, dark places, loud noises, strangers, and being separated from their parents. Although childhood fears are normal and to be expected, exaggerated or chronic fears should be evaluated by a professional.

Childhood aggression has been a topic of intense study in recent decades. Aggression, which appears by ages 2 or 3, may involve an intentional action to harm another (such as biting another child) or directed hostility to attain particular goals (such as taking a toy from another child). Fortunately, most children become less aggressive at about age 6. Preschoolers probably develop aggression in response to their egocentric perspective. Anyone or anything that frustrates egocentric children by preventing them from getting what they want is likely to trigger a hostile response. The male hormone testosterone may also explain why males are more likely than females to exhibit aggressive behavior. As with childhood fears, exaggerated or chronic aggression should be evaluated by a professional.

Ages 7 through 11 comprise **middle childhood.** Some authorities divide middle childhood into **early-middle** (ages 7–9) and **late-middle** (ages 10–11) periods. Like infants, toddlers, and preschoolers, these older children grow both physically and cognitively, although their growth is slower than it was during early childhood.

Physical Development in Middle Childhood

Physical development in middle childhood is characterized by considerable variations in growth patterns. These variations may be due to gender, ethnic origin, genetics, hormones, nutrition, environment, or disease. While children of this age group follow the same basic developmental patterns, they do not necessarily mature at the same rate. Most girls experience a preadolescent growth spurt around age 9 or 10, while most boys experience the same growth spurt around age 11 or 12. Children who do not receive adequate nutrition or medical attention may be at risk for stunted or delayed growth development. For example, children who live in countries where malnutrition is not a problem tend to be taller than children who live in countries where malnutrition is a problem.

Physical changes, brain and nervous system development, gross and fine motor skills, and health issues are important aspects of physical development during middle childhood as in previous developmental stages.

Physical changes
By the beginning of middle childhood, children typically have acquired a leaner, more athletic appearance. Girls and boys still have similar body shapes and proportions until both sexes reach **puberty,**

the process whereby children sexually mature into teenagers and adults. After puberty, **secondary sexual characteristics**—breasts and curves in females, deeper voice and broad shoulders in males— make distinguishing females from males much easier.

Girls and boys grow about 2 to 3 inches and gain about 7 pounds per year until puberty. Skeletal bones and muscles broaden and lengthen, which may cause children (and adolescents) to experience growing pains. Skeletal growth in middle childhood is also associated with losing the **deciduous teeth,** or baby teeth.

Throughout most of middle childhood, girls are smaller than boys and have less muscle mass. As girls enter puberty, however, they may be considerably larger than boys of the same age, who enter puberty a few years later. Once boys begin sexually maturing, their heights and weights eventually surpass the heights and weights of girls of the same age.

Brain and nervous system development

Brain and nervous system developments continue during middle childhood. More complex behavioral and cognitive abilities become possible as the central nervous system matures.

Early in middle childhood, a growth spurt occurs in the brain so that by age 8 or 9, the organ is nearly adult-size. Brain development during middle childhood is characterized by growth of specific structures, especially the **frontal lobes.** These lobes, located in the front of the brain just under the skull, are responsible for planning, reasoning, social judgment, and ethical decision making, among other functions. Damage to this part of brain results in erratic emotional outbursts, inability to plan, and poor judgment. The most anterior (front) portion of the frontal lobes is the **prefontal cortex,** which appears to be responsible for personality.

As the size of the frontal lobes increases, children are able to engage in increasingly difficult cognitive tasks, such as performing a series of tasks in a reasonable order. An example is assembling a mechanical toy: unpacking the pieces, connecting the parts, making the model move by adding a power source—a series of tasks that must be completed in the correct order to achieve certain results.

Lateralization of the two hemispheres of the brain, described in Chapter 6, also continues during middle childhood, as does maturation of the **corpus callosum** (the bands of neural fibers connecting the two cerebral hemispheres), and other areas of the nervous system. Interestingly, children achieve concrete operations around age 7 when the brain and nervous systems have developed a certain amount of neural connections. When these neural connections have developed, a child's ability to perceive and think about the world advances from an egocentric, magical viewpoint to a more concrete and systematic way of thinking. (Such cognitive developments are discussed later in the chapter.)

Motor skills

As defined in Chapter 6, **motor skills** are behavioral abilities or capacities. **Gross motor skills** involve the use of large bodily movements, and **fine motor skills** involve the use of small bodily movements. Both gross and fine motor skills continue to refine during middle childhood.

Children love to run, jump, leap, throw, catch, climb, and balance. Children play baseball, ride bikes, roller skate, take karate lessons, take ballet lessons, and participate in gymnastics. As school-age children grow physically, they become faster, stronger, and better coordinated. Consequently, during middle childhood, children become more adept at gross motor activities.

Children enjoy using their hands in detailed ways, too. From early in preschool, children learn and practice fine motor skills. Preschool children cut, paste, mold, shape, draw, paint, create, and write. These children also learn such skills as tying shoelaces, untying knots, and flossing their teeth. Some fortunate children are able to take music lessons for piano, violin, flute, or other instruments.

Learning to play an instrument helps children to further develop their fine motor skills. In short, along with the physical growth of children comes the development of fine motor skills, including the sense of competence and confidence to use these skills.

Health

Middle childhood tends to be a very healthy period of life in Western societies. The typical minor illnesses of early childhood—colds, coughs, and stomachaches—are likely to lessen in frequency in middle childhood. This improved resistance to common illnesses is probably due to a combination of increased immunity from previous exposures and improved hygiene and nutritional practices. Minor illnesses occur, but most illnesses do not require medical attention. As noted in Chapter 6, minor illnesses may help children learn psychological coping skills and strategies for dealing with physical discomforts.

Major illnesses for school-age children are the same as major illnesses for younger children: influenza, pneumonia, cancer, human immunodeficiency virus (HIV), and acquired immunodeficiency syndrome (AIDS). But **obesity,** or being 20 percent or more above one's ideal weight, is a special health problem that occurs during the school years. About 25 percent of school-age children in the United States today are obese, and the majority of these children go on to become obese adults. Obesity in adulthood is related to heart problems, high blood pressure, and diabetes. Although obese children are not at the same medical risks as obese adults, these children should master effective eating and exercise habits as early as possible to decrease the risk of later obesity- and health-related problems.

The majority of disabilities and deaths in middle childhood are the result of injuries from accidents. In the United States, nearly 22 million children are hurt in accidents each year. For children, the most common deadly accidents result from being struck by moving vehicles. Accidents may occur at, near, and away from home; therefore, adequate adult supervision is always important. Injuries occurring at school are usually the result of playground- and sports-related accidents. Consequently, children should always wear protective headgear and other safety gear when playing sports and riding bikes. Other causes of death in middle childhood include cancer, congenital defects, homicide, and deadly infections.

Cognitive Development in Middle Childhood

School-age children think systematically about multiple topics more easily than preschoolers. Older children have keener **metacognition,** a sense of their own inner world. These children become increasingly skilled at problem solving.

Piaget referred to the cognitive development occurring between ages 7 and 11 as the **concrete operations stage.** Piaget used the term *operations* to refer to reversible abilities that the child has not yet developed (see Chapter 6). By reversible, Piaget referred to mental or physical actions that can occur in more than one way, or in differing directions. While in the concrete operations stage, older children cannot think both logically and abstractly. School-age children are limited to thinking concretely—in tangible, definite, exact, and unidirectional terms—based on real and concrete experiences rather than on abstractions. Older children do not use magical thinking and are not as easily misled as younger children. Unlike preschoolers, school-age children know better than to ask their parents to take them flying in the air just like the birds do.

Piaget noted that children's thinking processes change significantly during the concrete operations stage. School-age children can engage in **classification,** or the ability to group according to features, and **serial ordering,** or the ability to group according to logical progression. Older children come to understand cause-and-effect relationships and become adept at mathematics and science. Comprehending the concept of **stable identity**—that one's self remains consistent even when circumstances change—is another concept grasped by older children. For example, older children understand the stable identity concept of a father maintaining a male identity regardless of what he wears or how old he becomes.

In Piaget's view, children at the beginning of the concrete operations stage demonstrate **conservation,** or the ability to see how physical properties remain constant as appearance and form change. Unlike preschoolers, school-age children understand that the same amount of clay molded into different shapes remains the same amount. A concrete operational child will tell you that five golf balls are the same number as five marbles, but the golf balls are larger and take up more space than the marbles.

Piaget believed that preoperational cognitive abilities are limited by **egocentrism**—the inability to understand the point of view of others. But egocentrism is not found in children in the concrete operations stage. By the school years, children have usually learned that other people have their own views, feelings, and desires.

As noted in Chapters 4 and 6, Piaget's model of cognitive development has come under increasing attacks in recent years. Modern developmentalists have frequently referred to experimental research that contradicts certain aspects of Piaget's theories. For example, cognitive theorists like Robert Siegler have explained the phenomenon of conservation as a slow, progressive change in the rules that children use to solve problems, rather than a sudden change in cognitive capacities and schemas. Other researchers have shown that younger and older children develop by progressing through a continuum of capacities rather than a series of discrete stages. In addition, these researchers believe that children understand far more than Piaget theorized. With training, for instance, younger children may perform many of the same tasks as older children. Researchers have also found that children are not as egocentric, suggestible, magical, or concrete as Piaget held, and that their cognitive development is largely determined by biological and cultural influences.

Memory

School-age children are better at the skill of remembering than are younger children. Experiencing more of the world, older children have more to draw upon when encoding and recalling information. In school, older children also learn how to use **mnemonic devices,** or memory strategies. Creating humorous lyrics, devising acronyms, chunking facts (breaking long lists of items into groups of three's and four's), and rehearsing facts (repeating them many times) help children memorize increasingly complicated amounts and types of information.

Youngsters may remember more when participating in **cooperative learning,** in which adult-supervised education relies on peers interacting, sharing, planning, and supporting each other. Developmentalists disagree on the relative value of cooperative learning versus **didactic learning,** in which a teacher lectures to students.

School-age children also begin to evince **metamemory,** or the ability to comprehend the nature of memory and predict how well one will remember something. Metamemory helps children sense how much study time is needed for next week's math test.

Childhood intelligence

Psychologists and other authorities are keenly interested in childhood intelligence. **Intelligence** is an inferred cognitive capacity that relates to a person's knowledge, adaptation, and ability to reason and act purposefully. Around the beginning of the twentieth century, Alfred Binet and Theophile Simon measured perception, memory, and vocabulary in children. These researchers divided a child's **mental age,** or level of intellectual attainment, by his or her **chronological age,** or actual age, to yield the child's **intelligence quotient (IQ).** Years later, the average IQ for a child was set at 100. Today, the two most famous IQ tests for children are the **Stanford-Binet Intelligence Scale** and the **Wechsler Intelligence Scale for Children (WISC),** both of which have been updated numerous times.

Some psychologists indicate that the multifaceted nature of intelligence necessitates a distinction between **basic intelligence** (academic IQ) and **applied intelligence** (practical IQ). For instance, Howard Gardner proposed that children exhibit **multiple intelligences,** including musical ability, complex movement, and empathy. Similarly, Robert Sternberg proposed the **triarchic theory** of intelligence, which states that intelligence consists of three factors: information-processing skills, context, and experience. These three factors determine whether cognition or behavior is intelligent.

An individual's intelligence, at least as measured by IQ tests, remains fairly constant throughout life. Yet considerable differences in IQ scores exist across a range of individuals. These individual differences are probably the result of some combination of genetics, home and educational environment, motivation, nutrition and health, socioeconomic status, and culture.

Critics repeatedly question the value of measuring intelligence, especially when the most commonly used testing instruments are inherently culture-specific. Critics point out that minorities score lower on IQ tests that are devised and standardized using white, middle-class subjects. These same minorities score higher on IQ tests devised and standardized using subjects from their own cultural background. Proponents of IQ tests suggest that it is possible to develop **culture-fair** (fair for all members in a culture) and **culture-free** (without cultural content) IQ tests, such as **Raven's Progressive Matrices Test.** This IQ test gauges the subject's ability to solve problems that are presented in unfamiliar designs. Proponents also claim that IQ scores effectively predict future academic performance—what these tests were originally designed to measure.

A great deal of uproar occurred in the 1970s in response to schools placing minorities into special education classes based on their IQ scores. These scores were obtained from culturally biased IQ tests. Today, IQ tests cannot be used as academic achievement or placement tests.

According to Erikson, the primary developmental task of middle childhood is to attain **industry,** or the feeling of social competence. Competition (athletics, daredevil activities) and numerous social adjustments (trying to make and keep friends) mark this developmental stage. Successfully developing industry helps a child build **self-esteem,** or an evaluative attitude toward the self, which in turn builds the self-confidence necessary to form lasting and effective social relationships.

Self-Concept in Middle Childhood

Most boys and girls develop a positive sense of self-understanding, self-definition, and self-control in middle childhood. Supportive and loving parents, teachers, and friends who make the children feel competent foster this type of development. When lacking skills in one area, children in this age group typically find another area in which to excel. Excelling in an area contributes to a child's overall sense of self-esteem and belonging in the social world. For example, a child who does not like math may take up piano as a hobby and discover a talent for music. The more positive experiences that children have excelling in one or more areas, the more likely that these children will develop the self-confidence necessary to confront new social challenges. Self-esteem, self-worth, self-regulation, and self-confidence ultimately form a child's **self-concept.**

Social Cognition in Middle Childhood

As children grow up, they improve in their use of **social cognition,** or experiential knowledge and understanding of society and the rules of social behavior. Children's use of **social inferences,** or assumptions about the nature of social relationships, processes, and others' feelings, also improves.

Peer relationships play a major role in fine-tuning social cognition in school-age children. Members of a peer-group are typically of the same race and socioeconomic status; many peer group members live in neighborhoods that are ethnically undiversified. Noncompetitive activities among peers, such as group projects in school, help children to develop quality relationships. Competitive activities, such as team sports, help school-age children to discover athletic talents as well as how to manage conflicts. Thus, older children learn about trust, honesty, and how to have rewarding social relationships when they interact with their peers. Eventually, a teenager's social cognition comes to fruition as long-term relationships based on trust are formed. Throughout these experiences, older children come to grips with the world as a social environment with regulations. In time, these children become better at predicting socially appropriate and workable behaviors. Other types of social cognition, including moral development and judgment, are covered in Chapter 10.

Family Relationships in Middle Childhood

Although school-age children spend more time away from home than they did as younger children, their most important relationships continue to be established at home. Children's family relationships normally include their parents, grandparents, siblings, and extended family members.

Middle childhood is a transitional stage—a time when parents begin sharing power and decision making with their children. However, because children have limited experiences upon which to draw when dealing with adult situations and issues, parents must continue to establish rules and define boundaries. An example of sharing power may be parents allowing their children to negotiate the amount of allowances. An example of not sharing power may be parents determining with whom their children may or may not play.

Children experience an increase in responsibility during this middle-childhood period. In addition to increased freedom, such as going unsupervised to a Saturday afternoon movie with their peers, children may be assigned additional household chores. These chores may include watching their younger siblings after school while their parents are at work. The majority of school-age children appreciate and enjoy their parents' acceptance of their more adult-like role in the family.

Discipline, while not necessarily synonymous with **punishment,** remains an issue in middle childhood. The question, which has been debated in social sciences circles for decades, becomes one of the role of discipline in teaching a child values, morals, integrity, and self-control. Today, most authorities agree that punishment is probably of less value than **positive reinforcement,** or the rewarding of acceptable behaviors.

Most modern families require two incomes to make ends meet. Consequently, some children express negative feelings about being latchkey kids or children whose parents leave them alone while they work. Children may question why their parents choose to spend so little time with them or become resentful at not being greeted after school by one or both parents. Straightforward and honest communication between parents and children may alleviate any concerns or upsets that arise. Parents may remind their children that the *quality* of time is more important than the *quantity* of time they spend together. In turn, parents should make sure that they do actually spend quality time with their children.

Friendships in Middle Childhood

Friendships, especially same-gender friendships, are prevalent during middle childhood. Friends serve as classmates, fellow adventurers, confidantes, and sounding boards. Friends also help each other to develop self-esteem and a sense of competency in the social world. As boys and girls progress through middle childhood, their peer relationships take on greater importance. For example, older children are likely to enjoy group activities, such as skating, riding bikes, playing house, and building forts. Peer relationships may also cause the development of concerns and worries over popularity and conformity.

As with same-age peers, friendships in middle childhood are mostly based on similarities. The awareness of racial or other differences may or may not affect friendships. Intolerance for those children who are not similar leads to **prejudice,** or negative perceptions about other groups of people. While peers and friends may reinforce prejudicial stereotypes, many children eventually become less rigid in their attitudes toward children from other backgrounds.

Peer Pressure

Many developmentalists consider **peer pressure** a negative consequence of peer friendships and relationships. Children most susceptible to peer pressure typically have low self-esteem. These children adopt the group's norms as their own in an attempt to enhance their self-esteem. When children are unable to resist the influence of their peers, particularly in ambiguous situations, they may begin smoking, drinking, stealing, or lying. Children who resist peer pressure are frequently unpopular.

Sexuality in Middle Childhood

In early childhood, sexual interest is an extension of pleasurable sensations and curiosity, not an outgrowth of eroticism. But by middle childhood, sexual interest becomes more goal-directed. Although Freud theorized that **sexual latency,** or lack of sexual interest, characterized middle childhood, today's developmentalists generally do not support Freud's position. Sexual curiosity and experimentation clearly continue and even increase in frequency during the grade-school years. Same-sex contact and play are also not unusual during middle childhood.

Preadolescence, often referred to as late childhood or the formative years, is the period of childhood between ages 10 and 11. At this time, children's fascinations with sexuality are coupled with hormonal and physical changes occurring in their bodies. With these changes comes self-consciousness about the body, especially in regard to being seen nude by friends and parents.

Ten- and eleven-year-olds normally continue to associate and play with same-gender friends, although they soon become aware of a heightened interest in members of the opposite gender. Growing sexual interests may take the form of off-color comments, jokes, and notes. Simultaneously, these children show an increasing interest in their own bodies, asking more pointed questions about the birds and the bees: puberty, sexual activity, and the basics of pregnancy and birth.

Most sexplay for 10- and 11-year-olds is among same-gender peers, even though much talk of the opposite gender takes place. Homosexual sexplay generally takes the form of showing off their genitals to each other and is not truly homosexual.

Preadolescent youngsters acquire and practice social and emotional skills to prepare for the social relationships that develop during adolescence. Groups of preteens frequently go shopping, to the movies, or to school dances and athletic events. Although no implication of genuine romance is apparent at this stage, some girls and boys develop crushes on each other and even date.

Stressors During Middle Childhood

Boys and girls in the grade-school years are not immune to the stressors of their worlds. Homework, difficulties making friends, changing neighborhoods and schools, working parents—these stressors and more are normal and expected during the course of growing up. Unfortunately, some children are exposed to more severe stressors, including divorce, physical abuse, and sexual abuse.

Divorce

Currently half of all marriages in the United States end in **divorce;** most of these marriages end within the first 10 years. Over 1 million children under age 18 are involved in divorces each year in the United States. As may be expected, the breaking up of the family unit is very stressful on the involved children, who may in turn feel depressed, guilty, angry, irritable, defiant, or anxious.

Children of divorce suffer. These children are confronted with many possible stressors: changes in their relationships with their parents, the daily absence of one parent, the possibility of remarriage, the presence of a stepparent, or the presence of stepsiblings. Children who are dissatisfied with one or both of their parents and/or their living situation before a divorce tend to have a hard time adjusting after a divorce.

Child physical abuse

Child physical abuse is the intentional infliction of pain, injury, and harm onto a child. Child abuse also includes emotional and psychological abuse, including humiliation, embarrassment, rejection, coldness, lack of attention, neglect, isolation, and terrorization.

Most modern experts believe child physical abuse is harmful to the emotional development of children. Adults who were physically and emotionally abused as children frequently suffer from deep feelings of anxiety, shame, guilt, and betrayal. If the experience was especially traumatic and emotionally painful (as abuse often is), victims may repress memories of the abuse and suffer deep, unexplainable depression as adults. Child abuse almost always interferes with later relationships.

Researchers have also noted a wide range of emotional dysfunction during, soon after, and long after physical abuse. Emotional problems may be exhibited as anxiety attacks, suicidal tendencies, angry outbursts, withdrawal, fear, and depression, among others. A decidedly negative effect of child abuse—a strong intergenerational pattern—is also worth noting. In other words, many abusers were victims themselves of abuse as children. In spite of the range and intensity of the aftereffects of child abuse, many victims are able to accept the abuse as a regrettable event, but an event that they may also leave behind.

Child sexual abuse

One emotionally damaging form of child abuse is **child sexual abuse.** Also known as **child molestation,** child sexual abuse occurs when a teenager or adult entices or forces a child to participate in sexual activity. Sexual abuse is perhaps the worst means of exploiting children imaginable. Ranging from simple touching to penetration, child sexual abuse is culturally forbidden in most parts of the world and is illegal everywhere in the United States. Experts estimate that as many as 25 percent of children in the United States are sexually abused each year.

Every state in the United States has laws against a specific type of child abuse known as **incest,** which is sexual activity between closely related persons of any age. Child sexual abuse is incest when the abuser is a relative. Incest occurs whether or not the relative is blood-related, which explains why stepparents can be arrested for molesting their stepchildren. Not all states have laws forbidding sexual activity among first cousins.

Contrary to a popular misconception, incest is less common than sexual abuse from a person outside the family, such as a family friend, teacher, minister, youth director, or scoutmaster. The perpetrators of incest are typically men; their victims are typically girls in their middle-childhood years. Oddly enough, the personality profiles of sexually molesting fathers suggest that few of these fathers have serious psychological problems. Instead, abusive behavior by the father seems to be a symptom of a dysfunctional-family system. However, abusers outside the family, called **pedophiles,** may be violent. Pedophiles are more likely than sexual abusers inside the family to be psychologically disturbed.

Education is the best preventive measure for child molestation. Parents should explain to their children how to avoid being touched inappropriately and what to do when touched in an inappropriate manner.

Adolescence—the transition period between childhood and adulthood—encompasses ages 12 to 19. It is a time of tremendous change and discovery. During these years, physical, emotional, and intellectual growth occurs at a dizzying speed, challenging the teenager to adjust to a new body, social identity, and expanding world view.

Physical Development in Adolescence

Perhaps no aspect of adolescence is as noticeable as the physical changes that teenagers experience. Within the span of a few years, a dependent child becomes an independent and contributing adult member of society. The start of adolescence also marks the beginning of Freud's final stage of psychosexual development, the **genital stage,** which pertains to both adolescence and adulthood.

Puberty is the time of rapid physical development, signaling the end of childhood and the beginning of sexual maturity. Although puberty may begin at different times for different people, by its completion girls and boys without any developmental problems will be structurally and hormonally prepared for sexual reproduction. The speed at which adolescents sexually mature varies; the beginning of puberty in both genders falls within a range of 6 to 7 years. In any grouping of 14-year-olds, for example, one is likely to see teenagers in assorted stages of development—some appearing as older children and others as fully mature adolescents. Eventually, though, everyone catches up.

Hormones are responsible for the development of both **primary sex characteristics** (structures directly responsible for reproduction) and **secondary sex characteristics** (structures indirectly responsible for reproduction). Examples of primary sex characteristics are the penis in boys and the uterus in females. An example of secondary sex characteristics is the growth of pubic hair in both genders.

During childhood, males and females produce roughly equal amounts of male (androgen) and female (estrogen) hormones. At the onset of puberty, the pituitary gland stimulates hormonal changes throughout the body, including in the adrenal, endocrine, and sexual glands. The timing of puberty seems to result from a combination of genetic, environmental, and health factors.

An early sign of maturation is the **adolescent growth spurt,** or a noticeable increase in height and weight. The female growth spurt usually begins between ages 10 and 14, and ends by age 16. The male growth spurt usually begins between ages 10 and 16, and ends by age 18.

Girls generally begin puberty a few years earlier than boys, somewhere around ages 11 to 12. Increasing levels of estrogen trigger the onset of puberty in girls. They grow taller; their hips widen; their breasts become rounder and larger; hair grows on the legs, under the arms, and around the genitals; the labia thicken; the clitoris elongates; and the uterus enlarges. Around the age of 12 or 13, most girls today begin **menstruating,** or having menstrual periods and flow. The onset of menstruation is termed **menarche.** At this time, females can become pregnant.

Increasing levels of the hormone testosterone trigger the onset of puberty in boys around ages 12 to 14. Boys become taller, heavier, and stronger; their voices deepen; their shoulders broaden; hair grows under the arms, on the face, around the genitals, and on other parts of the body; the testes produce sperm; and the penis and other reproductive organs enlarge. At this time, boys can impregnate sexually mature girls. Teenage boys may also experience the harmless release of semen during sleep, termed **nocturnal emissions** (wet dreams).

The resulting changes of puberty can have wide-ranging effects on teenagers' bodies. For both adolescent girls and boys, differences in height and weight, general awkwardness, emotional ups-and-downs, and skin problems (**acne vulgaris,** or pimples) are common. These and other changes, including the timing of sexual maturation, can be sources of great anxiety and frustration for the blossoming youth.

Health Issues in Adolescence

Adolescent health problems are often correlated with low socioeconomic status, poor diet, inadequate health care, risk-taking activities, personality issues, and a sedentary lifestyle. Yet the teenage years are typically healthy, although major health problems can emerge. Three possible major health problems include eating disorders, depression, and substance abuse.

Eating disorders

Eating disorders involve a preoccupation with food. The most common of these among teenagers is **obesity,** which is defined as a skin-fold measurement in the 85th percentile for one's height. Obesity carries with it the potential for social stigma, psychological distress, and chronic health problems. Approximately 15 to 20 percent of adolescents are obese.

A preoccupation with not becoming obese can lead to **anorexia nervosa,** or self-starvation. The typical anorexic is a model teenager who is obsessed with food—buying, cooking, and preparing it—but who eats very little herself. She is probably a perfectionist and has a distorted self-perception of her body, believing herself to be too fat. The anorexic is generally 20 percent under her ideal weight. As many as 1 percent of adolescent girls are anorexic, and 2 to 8 percent of them eventually die from starvation.

Related to anorexia is **bulimia nervosa,** a disorder that follows a pattern of binge-purge eating. After eating an enormous amount of food, bulimics vomit, take laxatives, or exercise vigorously to burn off recently consumed calories. Bulimics, like anorexics, are obsessed with food, weight, and body shape. Unlike anorexics, they maintain a relatively normal body weight.

Both anorexia and bulimia are far more common among females than males. They also cross all levels of society. The exact causes of these eating disorders are unknown.

Depression

As many as 40 percent of adolescents have periods of **depression,** a type of mood disorder characterized by feelings of low self-esteem and worthlessness, loss of interest in life activities, and changes in eating and sleeping patterns. Adolescent depression is often due to hormonal changes, life challenges, and/or concerns about appearance. More teenage females than males suffer from depression.

A real and tragic consequence of teenage depression is suicide. As many as 13 percent of adolescents report having attempted suicide at least once. Risk factors include feelings of hopelessness, suicidal preoccupation, a previous suicide attempt, having a specific plan to carry out the suicide, having access to firearms or sleeping pills, and stressful life events. As with adults, more teenage females attempt suicide, but more teenage males actually die from their attempts. Females use less violent methods (such as taking pills) than males, who tend to use more extreme and irreversible methods (such as shooting themselves).

Substance abuse

Some adolescents abuse substances to escape the pains of growing up, to cope with daily stresses, or to befriend peers who are part of a particular crowd. As alluring symbols of adulthood, alcohol and tobacco/nicotine are the easily available drugs of choice for adolescents. Alcohol is a depressant that acts to lower inhibitions while inducing a pleasant state of relaxation. Nicotine is a stimulant that allegedly produces a pleasant state of arousal. Marijuana, which contains **tetrahydrocannabinol (THC),** is the most widely used illicit substance in the United States. It produces a mild altered state of consciousness.

Drug use among teenagers is less common today than it was in the 1960s and 1970s, although many young people still smoke, drink, and use illegal drugs. In a 1989 study, 35 percent of high school seniors reported having had at least five drinks in a row at least once in the previous two weeks. Also, 24 percent of high school seniors reported occasionally using marijuana.

Cognitive Development in Adolescence

Most adolescents reach Piaget's stage of **formal operations** (ages 12 and older), in which they develop new tools for manipulating information. Previously, as children, they could only think concretely, but in the formal operations stage they can think abstractly and deductively. Adolescents in this stage can also consider future possibilities, search for answers, deal flexibly with problems, test hypotheses, and draw conclusions about events they have not experienced firsthand.

Cognitive maturity occurs as the brain matures and the social network expands, which offers more opportunities for experimenting with life. Because this worldly experience plays a large role in attaining formal operations, not all adolescents enter this stage of cognitive development. Studies indicate, however, that abstract and critical reasoning skills are teachable. For example, everyday reasoning improves between the first and last years of college, which suggests the value of education in cognitive maturation.

Intellectual development

According to Robert Sternberg's **triarchic theory,** intelligence is comprised of three aspects: **componential** (the critical aspect), **experiential** (the insightful aspect), and **contextual** (the practical aspect). Most intelligence tests only measure componential intelligence, although all three are needed to predict a person's eventual success in life. Ultimately, adolescents must learn to use these three types of intelligence.

Componential intelligence is the ability to use internal information-processing strategies when identifying and thinking about solving a problem, including evaluating results. Individuals who are strong in componential intelligence do well on standardized mental tests. Also involved in componential intelligence is **metacognition,** which is the awareness of one's own cognitive processes—an ability some experts claim is vital to solving problems.

analytic

Experiential intelligence is the ability to transfer learning effectively to new skills. In other words, it is the ability to compare old and new information, and to put facts together in original ways. Individuals who are strong in experiential intelligence cope well with novelty and quickly learn to make new tasks automatic.

creative

Contextual intelligence is the ability to apply intelligence practically, including taking into account social, cultural, and historical contexts. Individuals who are strong in contextual intelligence easily adapt to their environments, can change to other environments, and are willing to fix their environments when necessary.

practical

An important part of contextual intelligence is **tacit knowledge,** or savvy, which is not directly taught. Tacit knowledge is the ability to work the system to one's advantage. Examples are knowing how to cut through institutional red tape and maneuvering through educational systems with the least amount of hassle. People with tacit knowledge are often thought of as street-smart.

Moral development and judgment

Another facet of cognitive development is **moral development and judgment,** or the ability to reason about right and wrong. Lawrence Kohlberg proposed a theory of moral development with three levels consisting of six stages. The first level, **preconventional morality,** has to do with moral reasoning and behavior based on rules and fear of punishment (Stage 1) and nonempathetic self-interest (Stage 2). The second level, **conventional morality,** refers to conformity and helping others (Stage 3) and obeying the law and keeping order (Stage 4). The third level, **postconventional morality,** is associated with accepting the relative and changeable nature of rules and laws (Stage 5) and conscience-directed concern with human rights (Stage 6).

Moral development depends, in part, on the appearance of empathy, shame, and guilt. Internalization of morality begins with **empathy,** the ability to relate to others' pain and joy. Children in their first year begin to show signs of basic empathy in that they become distressed when those around them do likewise. Internalization of morality also involves shame (feelings of not living up to others' standards) and guilt (feelings of not living up to personal standards). Shame develops around age 2, and guilt develops between ages 3 and 4. As children mature cognitively, they evidence an increasing ability to weigh consequences in light of self-interest and the interest of those around them. Teenagers typically demonstrate conventional morality as they approach their 20s, although some may take longer to gain the experience they need to make the transition.

Research tends to support much of Kohlberg's model; however, the theory has been criticized on several counts. According to some experts, the model favors educated individuals who are verbally sophisticated. People may also regress in their moral reasoning or behave differently than their moral reasoning may predict. Culture, family factors, and gender affect the attainment of the higher levels of moral judgment; hence, Kohlberg's model has been criticized as limited in terms of certain cultures, family styles, and distinction between differences in male and female moral development.

An alternative to Kohlberg's model is that of Carol Gilligan. Gilligan proposed that men and women evince moral reasoning that is equally viable but that appears in different forms. She notes that men tend to be more concerned with justice, while women lean toward compassion. The differences most often appear in circumstances where men and women make moral judgments.

Similar to moral development is **religious development.** The three levels are the same as Kohlberg's: **preconventional** (fundamentalistic black-or-white and egocentric thinking based on religious laws and rules); **conventional** (conformity to accepted religious traditions and standards); and **postconventional** (relativistic gray thinking; the acknowledgment of religious contradictions, human interpretations, and the changeable nature of rules). This latter stage is reached when the person has moved out of Piaget's **concrete operations** and into **formal operations** or **postformal operations,** both of which involve extensive use of critical thinking skills. As with moral development, teenagers often evidence conventional religious thinking as they approach their 20s. Some move on to postconventional religious thinking during college, where they are exposed to a large number of different people and viewpoints.

Adolescence is the period of transition between childhood and adulthood. Developmentalists have traditionally viewed adolescence as a time of psychosocial storm and stress—of bearing the burdens of wanting to be an adult long before becoming one. Developmentalists today are more likely to view adolescence as a positive time of opportunities and growth, as most adolescents make it through this transition without serious problems or rifts with parents.

The Search for Identity in Adolescence

Freud termed the period of psychosexual development beginning with puberty as the **genital stage.** During this stage, sexual development reaches adult maturity, resulting in a healthy ability to love and work if the individual has successfully progressed through previous stages. Because early pioneers in development were interested only in childhood, Freud explained that the genital stage encompasses all of adulthood, and he described no special difference between adolescent and adult years.

In contrast, Erikson noted that the chief conflict facing adolescents at this stage is one of **identity versus identity confusion.** Hence, the psychosocial task for adolescents is to develop individuality. To form an identity, adolescents must define a personal role in society and integrate the various dimensions of their personality into a sensible whole. They must wrestle with such issues as selecting a career, college, religious system, and political party.

Researchers Carol Gilligan and Deborah Tannen have found differences in the ways in which males and females achieve identity. Gilligan has noted that females seek intimate relationships, while males pursue independence and achievement. Deborah Tannen has explained these differences as being due, at least in part, to the dissimilar ways in which males and females are socialized.

The hormonal changes of puberty affect the emotions of adolescents. Along with emotional and sexual fluctuations comes the need for adolescents to question authority and societal values, as well as test limits within existing relationships. This is readily apparent within the family system, where adolescents' need for independence from the parents and siblings can cause a great deal of conflict and tension at home.

Societal mores and expectations during adolescence now restrain the curiosity so characteristic of young children, even though peer pressure to try new things and behave in certain ways is also very powerful. Added to this tug-of-war are teenagers' increasing desires for personal responsibility and independence from their parents, along with an ever-growing, irresistible interest in sexuality.

Sexual Identity and Orientation in Adolescence

A part of discovering one's total identity is the firming of **sexual orientation,** or sexual, emotional, romantic, and affectionate attraction to members of the same sex, the other sex, or both. A person who is attracted to members of the other sex is **heterosexual.** A person who is attracted to members of the same sex is **homosexual.** Many use the term **gay** to refer to a male homosexual, and **lesbian** to refer to a female homosexual. A person who is attracted to members of both sexes is **bisexual.**

In the 1940s and 1950s, Alfred Kinsey and his associates discovered that sexual orientation exists along a continuum. Prior to Kinsey's research into the sexual habits of United States residents, experts generally believed that most individuals were either heterosexual or homosexual. Kinsey speculated that the categories of sexual orientation were not so distinct. On his surveys, many Americans reported having had at least minimal attraction to members of the same gender, although most had never acted out on this attraction. In short, Kinsey and colleagues brought to the attention of medical science the notion of heterosexuality, homosexuality, and bisexuality all being separate but related sexual orientations.

The etiology of heterosexuality, homosexuality, and bisexuality continues to elude researchers. Today's theories of sexual orientation fall into biological, psychological, social, and interactional categories.

Biological theories
Attempts to identify the specific physiological causes of homosexuality have been inconclusive. Traditional physiological theories include too little testosterone in males, too much testosterone in females, prenatal hormonal imbalances, prenatal biological errors due to maternal stress, differences in brain structures, and genetic differences and influences.

Psychological and social theories
Early childhood seems to be the critical period in which sexual orientation forms, suggesting that learning plays a part in causing homosexuality. Freudians have traditionally held that homosexuality is rooted in early childhood developmental conflicts, particularly the Oedipal conflict. Freudians believe homosexuality develops in response to troubled family relationships, an overly affectionate and dominant mother and a passive father, and/or the loss of one or both parents. However, these theories cannot explain why homosexuality occurs in individuals not coming from these types of families.

More recently, researchers have proposed that social-learning factors may be account for homosexuality. The sexual preference may develop when a child engages in early **cross-gender behaviors** (behaviors stereotypical of the other sex) or when a teenager's sexual drive emerges during a period of primarily same-gender friendships.

Interactional theories

Proponents of the **interactional theory** of homosexuality allege that sexual orientation develops from a complex interaction of biological, psychological, and social factors. John Money explains that prenatal hormones first act on the embryo's and fetus's brain, which creates a physiological predisposition toward a particular sexual orientation. During early childhood, social-learning factors influence the child, either facilitating or inhibiting the predisposition.

Sexuality in Adolescence

Adolescents struggle to find appropriate sexual outlets for articulating their desires. They participate in the same sexual activities as do adults, while usually in the absence of a committed and long-term relationship. Sexually active teenagers may think they are in love and date one person exclusively for extended periods, but they lack the level of maturity necessary to maintain intimate and loving relationships. Adolescent **promiscuity** may be indicative of emotional problems, including low self-esteem, dependence, immaturity, insecurity, or deep-seated hostility.

Teenagers find a variety of means to express themselves sexually. Most young people relieve sexual tension through masturbation, which by this age is an erotically motivated behavior. About 90 percent of males and 60 percent of females report having masturbated at least once by age 17. A second sexual expression for teenagers is mutual **petting,** or sexual activities other than intercourse. Petting is either heavy (below the waist) or light (above the waist). A third sexual outlet for adolescents is intercourse. The mechanics of sex are the same whether the participants are teenagers or adults. However, although the passion of sex may be present, the commitment and intimacy of a mature relationship are usually missing from the teenage experience.

According to U.S. statistics, which may vary, the average age for a first sexual intercourse is between 16 and 17. Complicating matters is the fact that sexually active adolescents either use contraception on an irregular basis, or they do not use it all. They also do not consistently take precautions against sexually transmitted diseases, even in this day of HIV and AIDS.

Five percent of adolescents experiment with homosexual activity with same-age partners, according to one national survey. These data probably do not represent the number of teenagers who are truly homosexual, because many adolescent homoerotic experiences are nothing more than sexual experimentation.

Homosexual teenagers may be hesitant to reveal their perceived preferences, or come out of the closet, because of society's and their peers' negative attitudes about homosexuality. These teenagers may avoid homosexual experiences or, if they have them, worry about their significance. Homosexual teenagers may also avoid disclosure for fear of being victimized by heterosexual teenagers. **Homophobia** involves negative remarks, social ostracizing, and threats; it can also involve **gay bashing,** or violently attacking homosexuals. People probably gay bash because of peer pressure and discomfort with their own sexual identity.

Problems resulting from adolescent sex

Perhaps the greatest potential problem faced by sexually active teenagers is an unplanned pregnancy. With so many teenagers refusing to use contraception consistently, teenage pregnancy has reached an unimaginable level in the United States. Each year, about 500,000 babies are born to adolescent mothers, who typically face many serious problems. Medically, pregnancy and childbirth during adolescence are risky to both child and mother. An adolescent girl's body is not fully developed, and she may not have access to adequate medical care or understand the importance of proper nutrition. Thus, she is at higher risk of having a miscarriage or a premature, low birthweight baby. The young mother also may die during childbirth.

Financially, many adolescent mothers are single and live in poverty. If they drop out of high school, they have limited earning power. With less money and more expenses, they are forced to accept welfare to support their children and themselves.

Teenage mothers who are married face similar problems. About 50 percent of teenage mothers are married, and according to statistics they struggle financially just as much as unwed teenage mothers. Not surprisingly, teenage marriages are plagued by poverty, again because of limited education and earning power. They are also highly susceptible to divorce because of their emotional and financial instability, some of which is due to immaturity and marrying for the wrong reasons.

Adolescent fathers may be eager to help their partners and offspring, but they usually do not have the means to do so. Like teenage mothers, teenage fathers lack the education and skills needed to find suitable employment. Of course, other teenage fathers do not want the responsibilities of marriage and parenting. In turn, they abandon the mother and child, who then must struggle even more to survive.

Sexually transmitted diseases (STDs) are another serious consequence of teenage sex. Each year, more than 3 million teenagers contract an STD—an alarming figure given the current HIV/AIDS epidemic. Such figures underscore the importance of why teenagers must understand the medical and social implications of their sexually activity.

Juvenile Delinquency in Adolescence

Peer pressure during adolescence is strong, sometimes so much so that teenagers engage in antisocial acts. **Juvenile delinquency** is the breaking of the law by minors. Two categories of delinquency are

- Minors who commit crimes punishable by law (such as robbery).

- Minors who commit offenses ordinarily not considered criminal for adults (such as truancy). Adolescents, especially males, are responsible for nearly half of crimes committed, especially against property.

The likelihood of a teenager becoming a juvenile delinquent is determined more by lack of parental supervision and discipline than socioeconomic status. **Adolescent rebellion** may grow out of tension between adolescents' desire for immediate gratification and parents' insistence on delayed gratification. Parents who are unwilling or unavailable to socialize younger children may be setting them up for problems later in adolescence.

While some offenders are sent to juvenile reform facilities, others are given lesser punishments, such as probation or community service. Still others are court-mandated to seek mental health therapy. Fortunately, most juvenile delinquents eventually grow up to be law-abiding and contributing citizens.

Development takes on new meaning in adulthood because the process is no longer defined by physical and cognitive growth spurts. Adulthood, which encompasses the majority of a person's life span, is marked instead by considerable psychosocial gains that are coupled with steady but slow physical decline.

Age clocks, or the internal sense of timing of physical and social events, determine the various life stages through which adults pass. Although people age at different rates, the majority of Americans, reinforced by social norms, pass through a series of predictable periods.

Perhaps the best-known stage theory of **adult development** is that offered by Daniel Levinson (see Chapter 1, Table 1-1). According to Levinson, the ages of 17 to 45 encompass **early adulthood,** which he divides into the **novice phase** (17–33) and the **culminating phase** (33–45). Levinson further divides the novice phase into the stages of **early adult transition** (17–22), **entering the adult world** (22–28), and **age-30 transition** (28–33). The **culminating phase** (33–45) consists of the **settling down** (33–40) and **midlife transition**(40–45) stages. As with any stage theory, these stages are only a guide for the development that normally occurs along a continuum. Not everyone progresses through each stage at exactly the same age.

Physical Development in Early Adulthood

The young adult years are often referred to as the peak years. Young adults experience excellent health, vigor, and physical functioning. Young adults have not yet been subjected to age-related physical deterioration, such as wrinkles, weakened body systems, and reduced lung and heart capacities. Their strength, coordination, reaction time, sensation (sight, hearing, taste, smell, touch), fine motor skills, and sexual response are at a maximum.

Additionally, both young men and women enjoy the benefits of society's emphasis on youthfulness. They typically look and feel attractive and sexually appealing. Young men may have healthy skin, all or most of their hair, and well-defined muscles. Young women may have soft and supple skin, a small waistline, and toned legs, thighs, and buttocks. Early in adulthood, neither gender has truly suffered from any **double standard** of aging: mainly, the misconception that aging men are distinguished, but aging women are over the hill.

With good looks, great health, and plenty of energy, young adults dream and plan. Adults in their 20s and 30s set many goals that they intend to accomplish—from finishing graduate school, to getting married and raising children, to becoming a millionaire before age 30. Young adulthood is a time when nothing seems impossible; with the right attitude and enough persistence and energy, anything can be achieved.

Health in Early Adulthood

Health and physical fitness during young adulthood are excellent. People in their 20s and 30s perform at exceedingly high levels on tests of endurance and stamina. They generally are at their best in terms of physical conditioning and overall sense of well-being.

Lest the picture seem too rosy, young adults are not completely immune to the effects of aging. The closer they get to age 40, the more physical limitations they begin to notice. In fact, many young adults detect a significant decrease in energy and increase in health concerns after 40. However, with proper diet and exercise, the physical and psychological vitality that accompanies young adulthood can be maintained well into the 40s and beyond.

The most common health problems of young adulthood are arthritis, asthma, diabetes, depression and other mental problems, hypertension (high blood pressure), multiple sclerosis, and ulcers. Other conditions, such as atherosclerosis (hardening of the arteries), cirrhosis of the liver, heart and lung problems, kidney problems, and a variety of other diseases, may not exhibit symptoms at this stage, but may already be causing internal damage. Two additional categories of health concerns during young adulthood are disabilities and sexually transmitted diseases.

Disabilities

A **physical disability** is any physical defect, change, difficulty, or condition that has the potential to disrupt daily living. It may be present from birth, result from disease or injury, or develop later. A physical disability, for example, may be the absence of a vital organ from birth, deafness that develops in childhood, a spinal cord injury from a motorcycle accident, or a chronic condition like multiple sclerosis. The most common physical disabilities in adults are cerebral palsy, blindness, deafness, spinal cord injuries, and a number of chronic medical conditions, such as diabetes.

Persons who evidence subnormal intellectual functioning and social skills beginning before age 18 are **developmentally disabled** (mentally retarded). By definition, the developmentally disabled have an IQ of 70 or less and do not demonstrate culturally appropriate levels of social skills, living skills, responsibility, communication, and personal independence for their age.

Adults with a **psychiatric disability** (mental illness, or psychological disturbance) struggle with mild to incapacitating emotional problems and limitations that are often caused by either anxiety or affective disorders. **Anxiety disorders** are characterized by bouts of anxiety and/or panic. The recurrence of such episodes prompts an avoidance of people, places, and things. In many cases, the individual knows his or her anxiety is irrational, but is unable to master it. A combination of drug and psychological therapies can effectively treat anxiety disorders, which can otherwise severely disrupt life activities.

Affective disorders (mood disorders) cause a person to experience abnormally high and/or low feelings. Although several types of mood disorders exist, the two most common are **unipolar depression,** marked by feelings of self-blame, sadness, guilt, and apathy; and **bipolar disorder** (manic-depressive), marked by alternating periods of depression and **mania** (extreme hyperactivity and elation). Most affective disorders are treatable with a combination of medications and counseling. Unipolar depression responds well to antidepressant medications; bipolar disorder, to lithium carbonate.

Sexually transmitted diseases

Certain sexually transmitted diseases (STDs) are caused by microscopic single-cell organisms known as **bacteria**. These organisms invade cells of the body, causing infection and disease. The most common bacterial STDs are gonorrhea, nongonococcal urethritis, nongonococcal cervicitis, chlamydia, and syphilis. Other STDs are caused by **viruses** — noncellular, microscopic particles that replicate themselves within invaded cells. Antibiotic medications are ineffective against them, making viruses very difficult or impossible to eliminate. The most common viral STDs are herpes, genital warts, and human immunodeficiency virus (HIV).

HIV is the virus that causes **acquired immunodeficiency syndrome (AIDS).** HIV does not directly cause death; rather it depresses the immune system of a victim to the point that infection and disease overwhelm the body's natural defenses. For HIV to attack human cells, it must first attach itself to special receptors on the cells' surface. Through several complex chemical reactions, cells attacked by HIV become factories that produce more viruses, which in turn attack more cells, which in turn become factories, and so on. Eventually the immune system becomes so depressed that almost any disease can easily overwhelm bodily defenses.

Based on medical research, HIV appears to be spread through the exchange of body fluids (blood, vaginal secretions, and semen), not through casual contact. The following are the most probable means of transmitting and contracting HIV:

1. Engaging in sexual activity that involves the exchange of fluids.

2. Receiving contaminated blood.

3. Using contaminated hypodermic needles.

4. Passing from an infected mother to her child during pregnancy or childbirth.

Although AIDS is presently incurable, treatments are available that slow progression of the disease by restoring immune system functioning. People can best protect themselves from HIV and AIDS by steering clear of high-risk activities and partners, as well as by practicing abstinence, using condoms during sex, and not sharing needles.

Death and young adulthood

Death rates during young adulthood are lower than during any other period of the life span. Except for HIV and AIDS in males and malignancies in females, the leading cause of death during the 20s and 30s is accidents. Death rates, however, double during each decade after age 35.

Socioeconomic status and race also have an impact on health and death rates. Less educated, urban, and poorer minorities tend to have the worst health and are at the greatest risk of premature death from violent crimes. For example, minority Americans between the ages 25 and 45 are more likely to die as a result of homicide than their white counterparts. Additionally, these same Americans are more likely to die of a drug overdose than whites of the same age.

Intellectual Development in Early Adulthood

Does intelligence increase or decrease during adulthood? This question has plagued psychologists for decades. Cross-sectional studies of IQ tend to show that young adults perform better than middle-aged or older adults, while longitudinal studies of IQ appear to indicate that people increase in intelligence through the decades, at least until their 50s. But the issue of intellectual development in adulthood is not so straightforward or simple. The results of the cross-sectional studies—younger adults, as a group, do better on IQ tests—may be due more to **cohort influences,** such as longer schooling or greater exposure to television than that enjoyed by the previous generation, than to aging influences. The results of the longitudinal studies—over time, persons do better on IQ tests—may be due to the effects of practice, increased comfort taking such tests, or the tendency for those who remain in the studies to perform better than those who drop out.

Attempts to measure IQ are complicated by the fact that there are different types of intelligence. **Crystallized intelligence** is the ability to use learned information collected throughout a lifetime, and **fluid intelligence** is the ability to think abstractly and deal with novel situations. Young adults tend to score higher on tests of fluid intelligence, while middle adults tend to score higher on tests of crystallized intelligence. Variables unique to young, middle, and older adults complicate any comparison of IQs among the groups. All things considered, the results of traditional IQ tests suggest that intelligence usually continues at least at the same level through young and middle adulthood.

Thinking patterns

Young adult thinking, especially in a person's early 20s, resembles adolescent thinking in many ways. Many young people see life from an idealistic point of view, in which marriage is a fairy tale where lovers live happily ever after, political leaders never lie or distort the truth, and salespeople always have consumers' best interests in mind.

People in their 20s have not always had the benefit of multiple life experiences, so they may still view the world from a naively trusting and black-or-white perspective. This is not to say that young adults do not question their world, challenge rules, or handle conflicts. These, and more, are normal developmental tasks that lead to realistic thinking and recognition of life's ambiguities. But until young adults reach that level of thinking, they may want absolute answers from absolute authorities.

Many young adults—particularly those who have attended college—develop the ability to reason logically, solve theoretical problems, and think abstractly. They have reached Piaget's **formal operations** stage of cognitive development. During this stage, individuals can also classify and compare objects and ideas, systematically seek solutions to problems, and consider future possibilities.

As young adults confront and work through the gray areas of life, some may go on to develop **postformal thinking,** or practical street smarts. Developing the **wisdom** associated with postformal thinking is a lifelong process, which begins in the teenage years and is fully realized in the older adult years.

Psychosocial development in adulthood consists of changes in lifestyles and relationships. According to Erikson, the primary task of early adulthood is to establish identity and **intimacy** (sharing one's total self with someone else) after wrestling with the **intimacy versus isolation** psychosocial crisis, which poses commitment to others opposite the possibility of self-absorption. Much psychosocial development occurring during this period is in conjunction with significant life changes, such as leaving home, finding a long-term romantic relationship, beginning a career, and starting a family.

Independence in Early Adulthood

An important aspect of establishing intimacy with a partner is first being able to separate from the **family of origin,** or family of procreation. Most young adults have familial attachments from which they are separating. This process normally begins during Daniel Levinson's **early adult transition** (ages 17–22), when many young adults first leave home to attend college or to take a job in another city. (For more information on Daniel Levinson's theory of life stages, see Chapter 1.)

By age 22, young adults have attained at least some level of attitudinal, emotional, and physical independence. They are ready for Levinson's **entering the adult world** (ages 22–28) stage of early adulthood, during which relationships take center stage. Moreover, dating and marriage are natural extensions of the eventual separating from the family of origin—a key process in becoming an adult. Early bonding and separation experiences, then, set the stage for later independence from the family and the ability to form healthy attachments.

Relationships in Early Adulthood

Love, intimacy, and adult relationships go hand-in-hand. Robert Sternberg proposed that **love** consists of three components: passion, decision/commitment, and intimacy. **Passion** concerns the intense feelings of physiological arousal and excitement (including sexual arousal) present in a relationship, while **decision/commitment** concerns the decision to love the partner and maintain the relationship. **Intimacy** relates to the sense of warmth and closeness in a loving relationship, including the desire to help the partner, self-disclose, and keep him or her in one's life. People express intimacy in the following three ways:

- **Physical intimacy,** or mutual affection and sexual activity.

- **Psychological intimacy,** or the sharing of feelings and thoughts.

- **Social intimacy,** or having the same friends and enjoying the same types of recreation.

The many varieties of love described by Sternberg consist of varying degrees of passion, commitment, and intimacy. For example, **infatuation,** or puppy love so characteristic of adolescence, involves passion, but not intimacy or commitment.

In addition to love and intimacy, a deeper level of sexuality is realized during young adulthood within the context of one or more long- or short-term relationships. While the maturity level of the participants affects adolescent sexuality, adult sexuality is fully expressive. Following are discussions of some of the most common types of adult relationships.

Singlehood

Today, many people are choosing **singlehood,** or remaining single, over marriage or other long-term committed relationships. Many singles clearly lead satisfying and rewarding lives, whatever their reasons for not marrying. Many claim that singlehood gives them freedom from interpersonal obligations, as well as personal control over their living space. As of the late 1990s, 26 percent of men and 19 percent of women in the United States were single adults.

Most singles date; many are sexually active. Typical sexual activities for singles are the same as those for other adults. Some singles are **celibate,** abstaining from sexual relationships.

Cohabitation and marriage
The two most common long-term relationships of adulthood are **cohabitation** and **marriage.** Cohabitors are unmarried people who live and have sex together. Of the more than 3 million Americans who cohabitate, most are between the ages of 25 and 45. Many individuals claim they cohabitate as a test for marital compatibility, but no solid evidence supports the idea that cohabitation increases later marital satisfaction. In contrast, some research suggests a relationship between premarital cohabitation and increased divorce rates. Other individuals claim that they cohabitate as an alternative to marriage, not as a trial marriage.

The long-term relationship most preferred by Americans is **marriage.** Over 90 percent of Americans will marry at least once, with the average age for first-time marriage being 24 for females and 26 for males.

Marriage can be advantageous. Married people tend to be healthier and happier than their never-married, divorced, and widowed counterparts. On average, married males also live longer than single males. Marriages seem to be happiest in the early years, although marital satisfaction increases again in the later years once parental responsibilities have ended and finances have stabilized.

Marriage can also be disadvantageous. Numerous problems and conflicts arise in long-term relationships. Unrealistic expectations about marriage, as well as differences over sex, finances, household responsibilities, and parenting are only a few potential problem areas. Severe problems may lead one or both spouses to engage in **extramarital affairs.**

Extramarital relationships

Nonconsensual extramarital sexual activity (not agreed upon in advance by both partners) is a violation of commitment and trust between spouses. People express various reasons for engaging in extramarital activities; in any case, such affairs can irreparably damage a marriage. Marriages in which one or both partners are unfaithful typically end in divorce. Some couples may choose to stay together for monetary reasons or until the children are grown.

Divorce

When significant problems in a marital relationship arise, some couples decide to **divorce,** or to legally terminate their marriage. About 50 percent of all marriages in the United States end in divorce, with the average duration of these marriages being about 7 years.

Both the process and aftermath of divorce are very stressful on both partners. Divorce can lead to increased risk of experiencing financial hardship, developing medical conditions (ulcers, for example) and mental problems (such as anxiety or depression), having a serious accident, attempting suicide, or dying prematurely. The couple's children and the extended families also suffer during a divorce, especially when disagreements occur over custody of the children. Most divorcees and their children and families eventually cope, and about 75 percent of divorcees remarry.

Friends

Friends play an important role in the lives of young adults. Most human relationships, including casual acquaintances, are nonloving in that they do not involve true passion, commitment, or intimacy.

According to Sternberg, **friendships** are loving relationships characterized by intimacy, but not by passion or commitment. In other words, closeness and warmth are present without feelings of passionate arousal and permanence. Friends normally come from similar backgrounds, share the same interests, and enjoy each other's company.

While many young adults experience the time constraints of going to school, working, and starting a family, they usually manage to maintain at least some friendships, though perhaps with difficulty. That is, as life responsibilities increase, time for socializing with others may diminish.

Adult friendships tend to be same-sex, nonromantic relationships. Adults often characterize their friendships as involving respect, trust, understanding, and acceptance—typically the same features of romantic relationships, although without the passion and intense commitment. Friendships also differ according to gender. Females tend to be more relational in their interactions, confiding their problems and feelings with other females. Males, on the other hand, often hesitate to share their problems and feelings, instead, seeking out common-interest activities with other males.

Friends provide a healthy alternative to family members and acquaintances. They can offer emotional and social support, a different perspective, and a change of pace from daily routines.

Establishing a Career in Early Adulthood

Another important activity during Levinson's **entering the adult world** (ages 22–28) and **age-30 transition** (ages 28–33) stages is establishing a career. This process normally begins in college or trade school, where young adults prepare themselves to enter the work force. Young adults commonly explore various career options before settling into one field of work. However, this does not mean that once a young adult chooses a particular career path that he or she will not deviate from it. On the contrary, more and more adults are switching vocations, not just changing jobs within a field. For example, a psychology professor may decide after years of teaching undergraduates to become a church pastor.

As dual-career marriages become more common, so do potential complications. If one spouse is unwilling to assist, the other spouse may become stressed over managing a career, taking care of household chores, and raising the children. And as attractive as equal division of parenting may seem, women in our culture still bear the primary responsibilities of child-rearing. Conflicting demands may partly explain why married women with children are more likely to leave their jobs than are childless and single women.

Still, multiple roles can be positive and rewarding. If they are of sufficient quality, these roles may be associated with increased self-esteem, feelings of independence, and a greater sense of fulfillment.

Starting a Family in Early Adulthood

As young adults enter the **culminating phase of early adulthood** (ages 33–45), they enter the **settling down** (ages 33–40) stage. By this time, their careers (at least the first one) has been established and a spouse found. If a couple have not already done so, they will probably decide to have one or more children and start a family.

Parenthood is generally thought to strengthen marriages, even though research indicates that marital satisfaction often declines after the birth of the first child. This decline may be due to such stressors as changes in usual roles and routines, increases in family responsibilities, and additional strains on finances. But marital satisfaction need not decline. If the marriage is already positive and the spouses share parenting duties equally, the stresses of parenthood may be minimized and not significantly interfere with marital happiness.

Regardless of the many joys of parenthood, new parents are not always prepared for the responsibility and time commitment that raising a child requires. This is especially the case when parenthood is accidental rather than planned, or when the child is difficult and prone to irritability and excessive crying. Some young adults also have troubles seeing themselves as parents, especially when they feel that an important activity, such as attending college, has been lost because of parenthood. Others, especially young women, may struggle with the issue of having to choose between the desire to pursue career versus staying at home to raise their children.

One growing trend is the postponement of marriage and child-bearing until people are in their 30s. Two advantages of waiting are that both partners are more emotionally mature and have a more stable relationship, both of which provide the necessary tools for weathering the storms of parenthood. **Nontraditional family** units represent another interesting trend. Examples of these include **blended families** (or stepfamilies, in which new family units are made up of children from previous marriages), **single-parent families,** and **same-sex families.** Meanwhile, some couples choose to remain childless. Couples who have children do not necessarily regard themselves as more fulfilled than couples who do not. The critical factor in a couples' satisfaction and happiness seems to be their ability to choose their lifestyles. Couples can learn more about family planning, conception, birth control, and other pregnancy options from organizations such as the Planned Parenthood Federation of America, National Right to Life Committee, and National Abortions Rights Action League.

According to Daniel Levinson, **middle adulthood** encompasses ages 45 to 65. This stage of the life span divides into the **new life phase** (ages 45–50), the **age-50 transition** (ages 50–55), and the **culminating phase** (ages 55–60), followed by the **late adult transition** (ages 60–65).

Physical Development in Middle Adulthood

Although no longer at the peak level of their young adult years, middle-aged adults still report good health and physical functioning, However, as a result of the passage of time, middle adults undergo various physical changes. Decades of exposure and use take their toll on the body as wrinkles develop, organs no longer function as efficiently as they once did, and lung and heart capacities decrease. Other changes include decreases in strength, coordination, reaction time, sensation (sight, hearing, taste, smell, touch), and fine motor skills. Also common among middle adults are the conditions of **presbyopia** (farsightedness or difficulty reading) and **presbycusis** (difficulty hearing high-pitched sounds). Still, none of these changes is usually so dramatic that the middle adult cannot compensate by wearing glasses to read, taking greater care when engaging in complex motor tasks, driving more carefully, or slowing down at the gym. Of course, people age at different rates, so some 40 year olds may feel middle-aged long before their 50-year-old counterparts. Most people, however, describe feeling that they have reached midlife by their mid-50s.

The biopsychosocial changes that accompany midlife—specifically, **menopause** (the cessation of menstruation) in women and the **male climacteric** (male menopause) in men—appear to be major turning points in terms of the decline that eventually typifies older adulthood. None of the biological declines of middle and late adulthood needs to be an obstacle to enjoying all aspects of life, including sex.

For example, too often society has erroneously determined that menopause inevitably means the end of female sexuality. However, while menopause gives rise to uncomfortable symptoms, such as hot flashes, headaches, irritability, dizziness, and swelling in parts of the body, post-menopausal women frequently report improved sexual enjoyment and desire, perhaps because they no longer worry about menstruation and pregnancy. For these same reasons, women who have undergone a **hysterectomy,** or surgical removal of the uterus, frequently report improved sexual response.

Men also experience biological changes as they age, although none is as distinct and pronounced as female menopause. Testosterone production lessens, which creates physical symptoms, such as weakness, poor appetite, and inability to focus on specific tasks for extended periods. However, this reduction in testosterone does not fully explain the psychological symptoms of anxiety and depression that may accompany middle adulthood, indicating that the male climacteric probably has more to do with emotional rather than physical events. During middle age, men are faced with the realization that they are no longer 20 years old and that they are not going to accomplish all they wanted to in life. They may also feel less sexually attractive and appealing, as they discover that seemingly overnight they have gained extra weight around the waist, are balding, and are feeling less energetic than they used to.

Because of society's emphasis on youthfulness and physical appearances, middle-aged men and women may sometimes suffer from diminished self-esteem. Women, for instance, experience the American **double standard** of aging: Men who are graying are perceived as distinguished, mature, and sexy, while women who are graying are viewed as being over the hill or past their prime. This double standard, coupled with actual physical changes and decline, does little to help middle adults avoid a **midlife crisis,** described more fully in Chapter 15.

Health in Middle Adulthood

Health during middle age is typically good to excellent. In fact, American middle adults are quite healthy, especially those who are college-educated, wealthier (with an annual income over $35,000), and white. The most common health problems experienced during middle age are arthritis, asthma, bronchitis, coronary heart disease, diabetes, genitourinary disorders, hypertension (high blood pressure), mental disorders, and strokes (cerebrovascular accidents). AIDS has also become an increasingly frequent health problem in this age group.

Stress, or the internal sense that one's resources to cope with demands will soon be depleted, is present in all age groups, although it seems to be unavoidable during middle age. Middle adults are faced with **stressors,** such as the challenges of raising a family, paying their mortgages, facing layoffs at the office, learning to use technology that is continually changing, or dealing with chronic health ailments.

All stressful events need not be negative **(distressors),** however. Psychiatrists Holmes and Rahe note that positive events **(eustressors),** such as marriage, vacations, holidays, and winning the lottery, can be just stressful as negative ones. They also indicated that the higher a person's stress levels, including the number of good or bad stresses being experienced, the more likely that person is to develop an illness within two years.

Resistance to stress, known as **hardiness,** varies from person to person. Hardiness is probably due to a combination of a person's **cognitive appraisal,** or interpretation, of the stresses, the degree to which he or she feels in control of the stresses, and his or her personality type and behavioral patterns. Some people, such as easygoing type B's, seem less bothered by stress and are thus better equipped physically to handle both negative and positive stresses than are other personality types, such as type A's, or more anxious people.

Most everyone considers death during middle age as being a premature occurrence. Even so, the death rate doubles during each decade after 35, and unlike death in adolescence and young adulthood, death during middle adulthood is more often the result of natural causes than accidents. Socioeconomic status and race also have an impact on health and death. Typically, less educated, urban, and poorer minorities have the worst health, frequently due to limited access to necessary medical care. The death rate for middle-aged black Americans is nearly twice that of their white counterparts.

Perhaps the place where stress is most keenly felt during middle age is at work. Middle adults may feel that their competence is in question because of their age, or middle adults may feel pressured to compete with younger workers. Research indicates that age has less to do with predicting job success than do tests of physical and mental abilities.

The most common sources of stress in the workplace include forced career changes, lack of expected progress (including promotions and raises), lack of creative input into decision making, monotonous work, lack of challenging work, inadequate pay, feelings of being underutilized, unclear procedures and job descriptions, conflicts with the boss or supervisor, lack of quality vacation time, **workaholism** (addiction to work), and sexual harassment. Long-term job stress can eventually result in **burnout,** a state of mental exhaustion characterized by feelings of helplessness and loss of control, as well as the inability to cope with or complete assigned work. Short of resigning, interventions to prevent burnout include using standard stress-reduction techniques, such as meditation or exercise, and taking longer breaks at work and longer vacations from work.

Most middle adults can be categorized as either successful in a stable career chosen during young adulthood or ready for a new career. Career changes are sometimes the result of reevaluation, or a **midcareer reassessment,** which can certainly be stressful. Such reexamination of one's vocation can come about for many reasons, such as feeling trapped in a career or even wanting to make more money. One recent trend, however, is for middle adults to leave high-paying professions to take on more humanitarian roles, such as ministers, social workers, or counselors.

The greatest source of job stress is **unemployment,** especially when termination comes suddenly. Besides wrestling with issues of self-esteem, unemployed workers must also deal with the financial hardship brought about by loss of income. As may be expected, unemployed persons who have alternative financial resources and who also cognitively reframe their situations tend to cope better than those who do not.

Intellectual Development in Middle Adulthood

As noted in Chapter 12, cross-sectional studies of IQ show young adults performing better than middle or older adults, while longitudinal studies of IQ tend to show the same people increasing in intelligence at least until their 50s. The results of the cross-sectional studies may be due more to **cohort influences:** the effects of practice, increased comfort taking such tests, and the tendency for those who remain in the studies to perform better than those who drop out.

Young adults score higher on tests of **fluid intelligence,** which is the ability to think abstractly and deal with novel situations, while middle adults improve over time on tests of **crystallized intelligence,** which involves using learned information collected throughout a life span. In summary, the results of traditional IQ tests imply that intelligence continues at approximately the same level at least into middle adulthood, and probably beyond.

Thinking patterns
Middle-age adult thinking differs significantly from that of adolescents and young adults. Adults are typically more focused in specific

---

directions, having gained insight and understanding from life events that adolescents and young adults have not yet experienced. No longer viewing the world from an absolute and fixed perspective, middle adults have learned how to make compromises, question the establishment, and work through disputes. Younger people, on the hand, may still look for definitive answers.

Many middle-age adults have attained Piaget's stage of formal operations, which is characterized by the ability to think abstractly, reason logically, and solve theoretical problems. Many of the situations facing adults today require something more than formal operations. That is, the uncertain areas of life may pose problems too ambiguous and inconsistent for such straightforward thinking styles. Instead, middle adults may develop and employ **postformal thinking,** which is characterized by the objective use of practical common sense to deal with unclear problems. An example of postformal thinking is the middle adult who knows from experience how to maneuver through rules and regulations and play the system at the office. Another example is the middle adult who accepts the reality of contradictions in his or her religion, as opposed to the adolescent who expects a concrete truth in an infallible set of religious doctrines and rules. Postformal thinking begins late in adolescence and culminates in the practical wisdom so often associated with older adulthood.

Adult learners

Does intellectual development stop at age 22? Not at all. In fact, in recent years, colleges and universities have reported an increased enrollment of **adult learners**—students age 25 or older. Of course, labeling this age group as adult learners is not to imply that the typical college student is not also an adult. Academic institutions typically identify those outside the 18–21 range as adults, because most have been working and rearing families for some time before deciding to enter or reenter college. Compared with younger students, adult learners may also have special needs: anxiety or low self-confidence about taking classes with younger adults, feelings of academic isolation and alienation, fears of not fitting in, or difficulties juggling academic, work, and domestic schedules.

Adults most often choose to go to college for work-related purposes. Many employers require workers to attain certain levels of education in order to qualify for promotions. Other workers go to college to learn new skills in preparation for another career. Additionally, certain organizations, such as state licensing boards, may require professionals to have a certain number of **continuing education** hours each year to maintain their licenses. Finally, adults may also return to college simply for personal enrichment.

Many adults today choose **distance education** as their primary learning method. Numerous educational institutions offer accredited courses, certificates, and undergraduate and graduate degrees by correspondence or via alternative learning formats, such as intensive study classes conducted one weekend per month, telecourses provided over the television, or virtual classrooms set up on the Internet. Some of the programs have minimal **residency requirements** (time actually spent on campus); others do not, which benefits adults in rural areas who use these alternative methods to access studies that were previously unavailable to them. Adult students who successfully complete external programs tend to be highly self-motivated and goal-oriented.

Erikson stated that the primary psychosocial task of middle adulthood—ages 45 to 65—is to develop **generativity,** or the desire to expand one's influence and commitment to family, society, and future generations. In other words, the middle adult is concerned with forming and guiding the next generation. The middle adult who fails to develop generativity experiences **stagnation,** or self-absorption, with its associated self-indulgence and invalidism.

Crisis in Middle Adulthood

Perhaps middle adulthood is best known for its infamous **midlife crisis:** a time of reevaluation that leads to questioning long-held beliefs and values. The midlife crisis may also result in a person divorcing his or her spouse, changing jobs, or moving from the city to the suburbs. Typically beginning in the early- or mid-40s, the crisis often occurs in response to a sense of mortality, as middle adults realize that their youth is limited and that they have not accomplished all of their desired goals in life. Of course, not everyone experiences stress or upset during middle age; instead they may simply undergo a **midlife transition,** or change, rather than the emotional upheaval of a midlife crisis. Other middle adults prefer to reframe their experience by thinking of themselves as being in the prime of their lives rather than in their declining years.

During the **male midlife crisis,** men may try to reassert their masculinity by engaging in more youthful male behaviors, such as dressing in trendy clothes, taking up activities like scuba diving, motorcycling, or skydiving.

During the **female midlife crisis,** women may try to reassert their femininity by dressing in youthful styles, having cosmetic surgery, or becoming more socially active. Some middle adult women try to look as young as their young adult children by dying their hair and wearing more youthful clothing. Such actions may be a response to feelings of isolation, loneliness, inferiority, uselessness, nonassertion, or unattractiveness.

Middle-aged men may experience a declining interest in sexuality during and following their male climacteric (male menopause). Fears of losing their sexual ability have led many men to leave their wives for younger women to prove to others (and to themselves) that they are still sexually capable and desirable. In contrast, middle-aged women may experience an increasing interest in sexuality, which can cause problems in their primary relationship if their significant other loses interest in sexual activity. This leads some middle-aged women to have extramarital affairs, sometimes with younger sexual partners.

The field of life-span development seems to be moving away from a **normative-crisis model** to a **timing-of-events model** to explain such events as the midlife transition and the midlife crisis. The former model describes psychosocial tasks as occurring in a definite age-related sequence, while the latter describes tasks as occurring in response to particular life events and their timing. In other words, whereas the normative-crisis model defines the midlife transition as occurring exactly between ages 40 and 45, the timing-of-events model defines it as occurring when the person begins the process of questioning life desires, values, goals, and accomplishments.

Relationships in Middle Adulthood

As in young adulthood, the two primary long-term relationships characteristic of middle adulthood are cohabitation and marriage. Cohabitors—unmarried people living together in a sexual relationship—often state their reason for cohabiting as either a trial for marriage or an alternative to marriage. The notion that cohabitation increases eventual marital satisfaction is without clear supporting evidence. Even so, middle adults often approach cohabitation from a more mature, experienced perspective than their younger counterparts. They may, for example, be divorced and not interested in remarriage.

By middle age, more than 90 percent of adults will have married at least once. Marital satisfaction is often described in terms of a U-curve: People generally affirm that their marriages are happiest during the early years, but not as happy during the middle years. Marital satisfaction then increases again in the later years, once finances have stabilized and parenting responsibilities have ended. Couples who stay together until after the last child has left home will probably remain married for at least another 20 years.

Divorce

Middle adults are not immune to problems in relationships. As noted in Chapter 13, about 50 percent of all marriages in United States end in divorce, with the median duration of these marriages being about 7 years. Those marriages that do last are not always happy ones, however. Unfortunately, some marriages ultimately dissolve, even when the spouses try to ensure that things work out.

The reasons for dissolving a relationship are many and varied, just as relationships themselves differ in their make-up and dynamics. In some cases, the couple cannot handle an extended crisis. In other cases, the spouses change and grow in different directions. In still others, the spouses are completely incompatible from the very start. However, long-term relationships rarely end because of difficulties with just one of the partners. Both parties are usually responsible for the factors that may lead to a relationship's end, such as conflicts, problems, growing out of love, or empty-nest issues that arise after the last child leaves his or her parent's home.

Love changes over time, and such changes may become evident by middle adulthood. The ideal form of love in adulthood involves three components: passion, intimacy, and commitment—termed

consummate love, or complete love. This variety of love is unselfish, devoted, and is most often associated with romantic relationships. Unfortunately, as Robert Sternberg has noted, achieving consummate love is similar to losing weight. Getting started is easy; sticking to it is much harder.

For many middle-aged couples, passion fades as intimacy and commitment build. In other words, many middle adults find themselves in a marriage typified by **companionate love,** which is both committed and intimate, but not passionate. Yet a relationship that has lost its sexual nature need not remain this way, nor do such changes necessitate the end of a long-term relationship. In fact, many middle adult couples find effective ways of improving their ability to communicate, increasing emotional intimacy, rekindling the fires of passion, and growing together. The understanding that evolves between two people over time can be striking.

For others, the end of passion signals the end of the relationship. Some people are so enamored with passion that they do not approach their loving relationships realistically. This is especially true for those whose relationship was based on infatuation or the assumption that so-called true love takes care of all conflicts and problems. When the flames of passion subside (which is inevitable in many cases) or times get rough, these spouses decide to move on to new relationships. Extramarital relationships are one consequence of marital unhappiness and dissatisfaction.

Interpersonal disagreements may increase as the couple becomes better acquainted and intimate. People who never learned how to communicate their concerns and needs with their spouse or how to work through conflicts are more likely to become separated or divorced. Most couples quarrel and argue, but fewer know how to work at resolving conflicts equitably. Troubled couples, however, can learn to communicate effectively through counseling or education, thus avoiding breakups and divorce.

Relationships that last

What is a sure predictor of a loving relationship's potential for growing or wilting? Long-term relationships share several factors, including both partners regarding the relationship as a long-term commitment; both verbally and physically expressing appreciation, admiration, and love; both offering emotional support to each other; and both considering the other as a best friend.

Essential to preserving a quality relationship is the couple's decision to practice **effective communication.** Communication is the means by which intimacy is established and nurtured within a relationship; it helps partners better relate to and understand each other. Communication helps them feel close, connected, and loved. And it creates an atmosphere of mutual cooperation for active decision making and problem solving. To communicate realistically is to have a satisfying and healthy relationship, regardless of the relationship's level of development.

Friends

In all age groups, friends are a healthy alternative to family and acquaintances. Friends offer support, direction, guidance, and a change of pace from usual routines. Many young adults manage to maintain at least some friendships in spite of the time constraints caused by family, school, and work; however, finding time to maintain friendships becomes more difficult for middle adults. During this period, life responsibilities are at an all-time high, so having extra time for socializing is usually rare. For this reason, middle adults may have less friends than their newlywed and retired counterparts. Yet where quantity of friendships may be lacking, quality predominates. Some of the closest ties between friends are formed and nourished during middle adulthood.

Children

As adults wait later to marry and start families, more and more middle adults find themselves rearing small children. This trend differs from the traditional American pattern of the last 100 years in which couples started their families in late adolescence or early adulthood. Despite the rising number of later marriages and older first-time parents, this traditional model of early marriage and parenthood still predominates, meaning that by the time most parents reach middle age, their children are at least of adolescent age.

Ironically, middle adults and their adolescent children are both prone to emotional crises, which may occur at the same time. For adolescents, the crisis involves the search for identity; for middle adults, the search is for generativity. These two crises are not always compatible, as parents try to deal with their own issues as well as those of their adolescents.

Parents respond to their children's adolescence in different ways. Some middle adults attempt to live out their own youthful fantasies—sexual and otherwise—through their children. They may try to make their teenage children into improved versions of themselves. For example, some parents may force their teenagers to take music lessons or make them join a sports team, while other parents may insist that their children attend a certain college or enter the family business.

Witnessing their children on the verge of becoming adults can also trigger a midlife crisis for some middle adults. The adolescent journey into young adulthood is a reminder to middle-aged parents of their own aging processes and inescapable settling into middle and later adulthood. Finally, for some families, teenagers may ignite so much tension at home that their departure to college or into a career can be a relief to parents. Other parents experience the **empty-nest syndrome,** or sense of aloneness, once all their children leave home.

In recent decades, some cultures have witnessed the phenomenon of grown children staying or returning home to live with their parents. Regardless of whether adult children choose to live with their parents for financial or emotional reasons, the experience can be difficult for all parties. Parents may be forced to delay getting reacquainted with each other as they manage a not-so-empty nest, and their adult children may have to adjust to social isolation and problems establishing intimate relationships. Adult children living at home also may be less likely to assume adult responsibilities, such as washing their own clothes or paying rent. This type of living arrangement tends to work best when the situation is mutually agreeable, is temporary, and when the children are less than 25 years old.

Middle-aged parents typically maintain close relationships with their grown children who have left home. Many parents report feeling as if they continue to give more than receive from relationships with their children, including helping with their finances or watching their pets when they are out of town. Still, most middle adults and their grown children tend to value their time together, even as their respective roles continue to change.

Parents

Most middle adults characterize the relationship with their parents as affectionate. Indeed, a strong bond is often present between related middle and older adults. Although the majority of middle adults do not live with their parents, contacts are usually frequent and positive. And perhaps for the first time, middle adults are able to see their parents as the fallible human beings that they are.

One issue facing middle adults is that of caring for their aging parents. In some cases, adults, who expected to spend their middle-age years traveling and enjoying their own children and grandchildren, instead find themselves taking care of their ailing parents. Some parents are completely independent of their adult children's support, while others are partially independent of their children; and still others are completely dependent. Children of dependent parents may assist them financially (paying their bills), physically (bringing them into their homes and caring for them), and emotionally (as a source of human contact as the parents' social circle diminishes). Daughters and daughters-in-law are the most common caretakers of aging parents and in-laws.

Support groups and counseling resources are available for adults caring for their older parents. These forms of assistance typically provide information, teach caregiver skills, and offer emotional support. Other programs, such as Social Security and Medicare, are designed to ease the financial burdens of older adults and their caregivers.

The middle adult's reaction to the death of one or both parents is normally intense and painful, as it is for individuals of all stages of the life span. For the middle adult, the death of a parent ends a lifelong relationship. Additionally, it may be wake-up call to live life to its fullest and to mend broken relationships while loved ones are still alive. Finally, a parent's death is a reminder of one's own mortality.

Even though the death of a parent is never welcome, some long-term adult caretakers express ambivalent feelings about the event. The grown children of parents dying of a lingering illness, for example, usually do not want to see their loved ones suffer—even if alleviation means death. These children may find themselves hoping simultaneously for a cure and for a peaceful release from the pain that their parent is experiencing.

Daniel Levinson depicts the **late adulthood** period as those years that encompass age 65 and beyond. Other developmental psychologists further divide later adulthood into **young-old** (ages 65–85) and **old-old** (ages 85 and beyond) stages.

Today, 13 percent of the population is over the age of 65, compared with 3 percent at the beginning of this century. This dramatic increase in the demographics of older adulthood has given rise to the discipline of **gerontology,** or the study of old age and aging. **Gerontologists** are particularly interested in confronting **ageism,** or prejudice and discrimination against older adults.

Physical Development in Late Adulthood

Aging inevitably means physical decline, some of which may be due to lifestyle, such as poor diet and lack of exercise, rather than illness or the aging process. Energy reserves dwindle. Cells decay. Muscle mass decreases. The immune system is no longer as capable as it once was in guarding against disease. Body systems and organs, such as the heart and lungs, become less efficient. Overall, regardless of people's best hopes and efforts, aging translates into decline.

Even so, the speed at which people age, as well as how aging affects their outlook on life, varies from person to person. In older adulthood, people experience both **gains** and **losses.** For instance, while energy is lost, the ability to conserve energy is gained. Age also brings understanding, patience, experience, and wisdom—qualities that improve life regardless of the physical changes that may occur.

Aging in late adulthood profoundly affects appearance, sensation, and motor abilities. An older adult's appearance changes as wrinkles appear and the skin becomes less elastic and thin. Small blood vessels break beneath the surface of the skin, and warts, skin tags, and age spots (liver spots) may form on the body. Hair thins and turns gray as melanin decreases, and height lessens perhaps by an inch or two as bone density decreases. The double standard of aging applies to men and women in older adulthood just as it did in middle adulthood. Older men may still be seen as distinguished, while older women are labeled as grandmotherly, over the hill, and past the prime of life.

During late adulthood, the senses begin to dull. With age, the lenses of the eye discolor and become rigid, interfering with the perception of color and distance and the ability to read. Without corrective glasses, nearly half the elderly population would be legally blind. Hearing also diminishes, especially the ability to detect high-pitched sounds. As a result, the elderly may develop suspiciousness or even a mild form of **paranoia**—unfounded distrustfulness—in response to not being able to hear well. They may attribute bad intentions to those whom they believe are whispering or talking about them, rather than correctly attributing their problems to bad hearing. Hearing problems can be corrected with hearing aids, which are widely available.

The sense of taste remains fairly intact into old age, even though the elderly may have difficulty distinguishing tastes within blended foods. By old age, however, the sense of smell shows a marked decline. Both of these declines in sensation may be due to medications, such as antihypertensives, as well as physical changes associated with old age.

In addition to changes in appearance and the dulling of the senses, reflexes slow and fine motor abilities continue to decrease with old age. By late adulthood, most adults have noticed a gradual reduction in their response time to spontaneous events. This is especially true of older adults who drive. While routine maneuvers on familiar streets may pose fewer problems than novel driving situations, older adults' reaction times eventually decline to the point that operating a vehicle is too hazardous. However, many elderly are hesitant to give up driving because the sacrifice would represent the end of their personal autonomy and freedom.

Generally, older adults score lower overall on tests of manual dexterity than do younger adults. Older adults may find that their fine motor skills and performance speed decrease in some areas but not in others. For instance, an elderly lifelong pianist may continue to exhibit incredible finger dexterity at the keyboard, but may at the same time find that taking up needlepoint as a hobby is too difficult.

Aging also takes its toll on sexuality. Older women produce less vaginal lubrication, and the vagina becomes less stretchable because of reduced levels of female hormones. Older men are less able to attain erections and orgasms than are younger men. This may be due to reduced levels of testosterone and fewer secretions from the accessory sex glands. Likewise, older men have less urge to ejaculate, and their **refractory periods,** or the waiting time before they can regain an erection, may last longer.

Physical changes in sexual ability don't have to prevent older adults from enjoying sex. Although fewer in orgasmic contractions, orgasm continues to be a pleasurable event for both genders. In fact, older people may find sex to be slower and more sensual. Older women relax because they no longer fear pregnancy, older men's erections last longer, and neither is as anxious, insecure, or hurried as they may have been decades before. Regular sexual practice also may help older adults maintain their sexual interest and prowess.

Health in Late Adulthood

Although the average life expectancy is 79 for females and 72 for males, older adulthood can easily extend 20 years or more beyond these figures. As older adults age, most report increasing health problems. Even so, only about 5 percent of adults over age 65 and 25 percent of those over age 85 live in nursing homes, foster care (where elderly people live with a family licensed by the state to care for aging adults), or other long-term care facilities. With medical advances and continued improvements in health-care delivery, the older population is expected to increase in its numbers and report better health. Estimates are that within the next 30 years, one out of every five Americans will be an older adult.

Although most older adults have at least one chronic health problem, such ailments need not pose limitations on activities well into the adults' 80s and beyond. The most common medical concerns during older adulthood are arthritis and rheumatism, cancer, cataracts of the eyes, dental problems, diabetes, hearing and vision problems, heart disease, hypertension, and orthopedic injuries. Because the elderly are at greater risk of losing their balance and falling, hip fractures and breakages are particularly common and dangerous in this age group.

Contracting colds and flus can have especially serious repercussions for the elderly. This is due, in part, to the reduced capacity of older adults' body organs and immune system to fight disease. Unfortunate, but not uncommon, is the following scenario: An elderly person falls at home and breaks a hip bone, undergoes successful hip-replacement surgery, and then dies two weeks later from postoperative pneumonia or other infections because of reduced reserve capacity and inability to recover from infection.

Inadequate nutrition and the misuse of medication also may be implicated in older adults who suffer from poor health. By the time adults reach age 65, they need 20 percent fewer calories than they did in their youth, but they still need the same amount of nutrients. This may explain, in part, why so many older Americans are overweight but undernourished. Additionally, cooking becomes a hassle for many older adults, and they find it easier to eat fast food, junk food, or nothing at all. Furthermore, many elderly unintentionally overuse prescription medication or combine medications that, when used together, produce toxic effects. As the body ages and potentially becomes more sensitive to the effects of prescription medications, drug dosages should be carefully monitored and assessed by a physician. Many elderly who have been hospitalized in near-death condition begin to recover as soon as their medications are reduced or stopped.

Life expectancy can be prolonged through exercise. Older adults who have kept active, remained fit, and eaten wholesome foods throughout their lives tend to fare better than those who have not. This should be a lesson to younger adults who have an opportunity to modify their health habits early in life.

Dementia and Alzheimer's disease

The mental, emotional, and behavioral problems typically encountered by older adults are depression, anxiety, and **dementia** (mental deterioration, also known as **organic brain syndrome.** Poor nutrition, inadequate sleep, metabolic problems, and strokes may cause dementia, which affects 4 percent of those over age 65. (Dementia due to strokes is sometimes termed **multi-infarct dementia.**) Older adults with dementia experience forgetfulness, confusion, and personality changes. Many people use the term **senility** to refer to dementia, which is incorrect. Senility does not have a precise or actual medical meaning; it is an overused and nonspecific term, like the word neurosis.

Similar in symptoms to dementia is **Alzheimer's disease,** an irreversible degenerative brain disorder that can affect as many as 50 percent of older adults over age 85 and eventually results in death. Early symptoms of Alzheimer's disease include agitation, confusion, difficulty concentrating, loss of memory and orientation, and trouble speaking. Later symptoms include the inability to use or understand language, and total loss of control over bodily functions. Unfortunately, Alzheimer's is still a mystery to doctors and other scientists. In fact, the only certain diagnostic procedure for Alzheimer's disease is the analysis of autopsied brain tissue. The exact causes of Alzheimer's disease continue to elude researchers, although some suspect that genetics and malfunctions in enzyme activity may play a role.

Intelligence and Memory in Late Adulthood

People often fear that aging will cause their intellect to disappear, giving way to cognitive impairment and irrationality. However, intellectual decline is not an inevitable consequence of aging. Research does not support the stereotypic notion of the elderly losing general cognitive functioning or that such loss, when it does occur, is necessarily disruptive. Older adults tend to learn more slowly and perform less well on tasks involving imagination and memorization than do younger adults, but what older adults may be lacking in terms of specific mental tasks, they make up for in **wisdom,** or expert and practical knowledge based on life experience.

Many older adults complain about not being able to remember things as well as they once could. Memory problems seem to be due to sensory storage problems in the **short-term** rather than **long-term** memory processes. That is, older adults tend to have much less difficulty recalling names and places from long ago than they do acquiring and recalling new information.

Practice and repetition may help minimize the decline of memory and other cognitive functions. Researchers have found that older adults can improve their scores on assorted tests of mental abilities with only a few hours of training. Working puzzles, having hobbies, learning to use a computer, and reading are a few examples of activities or approaches to learning that can make a difference in older adults' memory and cognitive functions.

Recent decades have witnessed older adults' growing interest in continuing their education. In fact, many colleges and community centers offer classes for free or at a significant discount for senior citizens. Although keeping up with a class of 20 year olds may be a challenge, older adults can learn new information if it is presented clearly, slowly, and over a period of time. Older adults also can enrich the learning process for others through the insight and wisdom they've gained from life experience. Younger students often remark that they appreciate the practical perspective that their older colleagues offer.

Older adults who have kept their minds active and fit continue to learn and grow, but perhaps more gradually than their younger colleagues. Patience and understanding (on the part of both the elderly and their significant others), memory training, and continued education are important for maintaining mental abilities and the quality of life in the later years.

Erik Erikson, who took a special interest in this final stage of life, concluded that the primary psychosocial task of late adulthood (65 and beyond) is to maintain **ego integrity** (holding on to one's sense of wholeness), while avoiding **despair** (fearing there is too little time to begin a new life course). Those who succeed at this final task also develop wisdom, which includes accepting without major regrets the life that one has lived, as well as the inescapability of death. However, even older adults who achieve a high degree of integrity may feel some despair at this stage as they contemplate their past. No one makes it through life without wondering if another path may have been happier and more productive.

Theories of Aging

Two major theories explain the psychosocial aspects of aging in older adults. **Disengagement theory** views aging as a process of mutual withdrawal in which older adults voluntarily slow down by retiring, as expected by society. Proponents of disengagement theory hold that mutual social withdrawal benefits both individuals and society. **Activity theory,** on the other hand, sees a positive correlation between keeping active and aging well. Proponents of activity theory hold that mutual social withdrawal runs counter to traditional American ideals of activity, energy, and industry. To date, research has not shown either of these models to be superior to the other. In other words, growing old means different things for different people. Individuals who led active lives as young and middle adults will probably remain active as older adults, while those who were less active may become more disengaged as they age.

As older adults approach the end of their life span, they are more apt to conduct a **life review.** The elderly may reminisce for hours on end, take trips to favorite childhood places, or muse over photo albums and scrapbooks. Throughout the process, they look back to try to find the meaning and purpose that characterized their lives. In their quest to find life's meaning, older adults often have a vital need to share their reminisces with others who care, especially family.

Relationships in Late Adulthood

Given increases in longevity, today's older adults face the possibility of acquiring and maintaining relationships far longer than during any other time in modern history. For instance, nearly 1 in 10 adults over the age of 65 has a child who is also within the older adult age range. Nurturing long-term family relationships can be both rewarding and challenging. While middle and older adults may enjoy the peaceful relationships that develop over the decades in place of sibling rivalry, younger adults may feel the strain of trying to care for their aging and ailing parents, grandparents, and other relatives. Even so, most young people report that they have satisfying relationships with their older family members.

Marriage and family
Older adult marriages and families are sometimes referred to as retirement marriages or retirement families. In such families, the following demographics are typical: The average age of the wife is 68, and the husband, 71; they have been married for over 40 years and report high levels of marital satisfaction; they have three grown children, the oldest being about 40; and 20 percent of the husbands and 4 percent of the wives continue to work, even though they consider themselves retired. For these families, the typical household finances are less than in earlier stages of the life span.

By far the most devastating event in older adult marriages is **widowhood,** or the disruption of marriage due to death of the spouse. Nearly 3 percent of men (widowers) and 12 percent of women (widows) in the United States are widowed. In the 75 and older age group, approximately 25 percent of men and 66 percent of women are widowed.

One common complaint of widows and widowers is the difficulty they experience finding a new spouse or partner. This is especially true of widows, who must contend with the social stigmas of being old and asexual in a youth-oriented society. Widows tend to outnumber widowers in retirement communities, assisted living facilities, and nursing homes.

Late adulthood and sexuality
Perhaps no other topic lends itself to misconception more than that of sexuality among the elderly. The notion that a dramatic reduction in the frequency of sexual activity occurs after middle age is groundless. The best predictor of future sexual behavior is present and past sexual behavior: The more sexually active a person is and was in earlier years, the more active she or he will likely be in later years.

Setting aside unfounded expectations about sex and the elderly, the main sexual problem that older adults face is finding a fitting partner. This is a special problem for older women, who—with a greater life expectancy than older men—find themselves with few or no options for potential sex partners. Furthermore, contemporary society typically accepts older men marrying younger women, but not the reverse, which leaves older women with one option—celibacy.

Aging rarely means that youthful activities come to a halt, just that they must be approached more creatively. This shift of pace and perspective is true of jogging (where running replaces sprinting) and golfing (where carting replaces walking), as well as of sex (where patience and understanding replace fast and furious lovemaking). In none of these instances does aging have to interfere with enjoying the activity.

Even when misconceptions are challenged, however, society still holds negative ideas about sex in late adulthood. Many people see elderly sex as passionless, sickly, and dull. To help put an end to these attitudes, researcher Edward Brecher recommended that sexually active older adults be more open about their sexuality. In this way, younger members of society can see what joys these later years can hold for loving, healthy adults.

Relationships with adult children

The majority of older Americans—some 80 to 90 percent—have grown children, and enjoy frequent contact with them. Contrary to popular misconceptions, while the elderly enjoy these contacts, they do not want to live with their grown children. Instead, they want to live in their own homes and remain independent for as long as possible. They typically would rather move into a private room in an assisted living facility or group home than move in with their children. At any one time, only about 5 percent of adults over age 65 live in an institution; the other 95 percent either live alone or with a spouse, other relative, or a nonrelative. People over 65 are, however, more likely than any other age group to reside in an institutionalized setting at some point in their later lives. Over 75 percent of institutionalized older adults live within an hour's drive of one of their children.

As for the quality of the relationships between older adults and their grown children, most research suggests that the elderly rate their experiences as positive. This response is most likely to reflect the older adults' good health, and the common interests (for instance, church or hobbies) and similar views (such as politics, religion, child-rearing) that they share with their children. The elderly do not necessarily rate frequent contacts with their children as positive when these take place as a result of long-term illness or family problems (such as a daughter's divorce).

Elderly abuse

One particularly disturbing aspect of older adulthood is the potential for **elderly abuse,** or the neglect and/or physical and emotional abuse of dependent elderly persons. Neglect may take the form of care-givers withholding food or medications, not changing bed linens, or failing to provide proper hygienic conditions. Physical abuse may include striking, shoving, shaking, punching, or kicking the elderly, while emotional abuse may consist of verbal threats, swearing, and insults. In the United States, an estimated 5 percent of older adults are abused each year.

Elderly abuse can occur in institutions, but it more commonly happens in the homes of the older person's spouse, children, or grandchildren. The typical victim is an older adult who is in poor health and who lives with someone else. In fact, the person who lives alone is at low risk of becoming a victim of this form of abuse. Both victims and abusers require treatment, whether individual, family, or group therapy. The main goal, however, is to ensure the safety of the elderly victim. Many licensed professionals, such as clinical psychologists, are required by law to report known cases of elderly abuse to the authorities.

Relationships with grandchildren

Because people become grandparents at an average age of 52 for men and 50 for women, grandparenting is hardly restricted to older adults. Older adults, however, often have more free time for their grandchildren. Middle adults often have less time because of work and other responsibilties.

Although often idealized, grandparenting is a role that takes on different dimensions with individual situations, and the quality of grandparent-grandchild relationships varies across families. Generally, the majority of grandparents report having warm and loving relationships with their grandchildren. Besides helping their grandchildren develop an appreciation for the past, positive grandparenting helps older adults avoid isolation and dependence while finding additional meaning and purpose in life. Grandparenting also facilitates personality development in later life by allowing older adults opportunities to reexamine and rework the tasks of earlier psychosocial stages.

Friendships

Having close friends in later life, like any other period, is consistently associated with happiness and satisfaction. Friends provide support, companionship, and acceptance, conditions that are crucial to most older adults' sense of self-esteem and self-worth. Friendships provide opportunities to trust, confide, and share mutually enjoyed activities. They also seem to protect against stress, physical and mental problems, and premature death.

Because older men are more likely to rely on their wives for companionship, older women typically enjoy a wider circle of close friends. Older men, however, develop more other-gender friendships. On the other hand, when older women can find available men with whom to be friends, they may be hesitant to become too close. These women may worry about what others are thinking, as they do not want to appear improper or forward.

Work and Retirement in Late Adulthood

Older adults who are still working are typically committed to their work, are productive, report high job satisfaction, and rarely change jobs. However, fewer older adults are working today than were in the 1950s. In fact, only a small portion of adults age 70 and older are in the work force. With Social Security benefits beginning as early as age 62, some companies have opted to offer early retirement incentives that permit employees to leave their positions without penalizing them before the regular retirement age. Then the companies can hire less-experienced and less-expensive employees. Other companies encourage their older workers to continue working part-time. While many older adults continue to work for pay, most retire between the ages of 65 and 70.

Retirement is a major transition of late adulthood. The retired person must eventually accept a more leisurely life, whether desired or not. He or she must also continue to live in a worker's world, in which retirees are viewed as spent or devalued. Indeed, the psychological impact of retirement on older adults can be significant. Many must contend with feelings of depression, uselessness, and low self-esteem.

People who are in good health, are better educated, have few or no financial worries, have adequate family and social networks, and are satisfied with life usually look forward to retirement. Retirees may choose to spend their free time volunteering for charities, traveling, taking classes, or engaging in hobbies. The least satisfied retirees are those who never planned for retirement, have limited income, have few or no extracurricular activities, and who stay home day after day with nothing substantial to occupy their time.

About Thanatology

At the end of the human life span, people face the issues of dying and **death** (the permanent cessation of all life functions). North American society in recent years has witnessed an increased interest in the **thanatology,** or the study of death and dying. **Thanatologists** examine all aspects of death, including biological (the cessation of physiological processes), psychological (cognitive, emotional, and behavioral responses), and social (historical, cultural, and legal issues).

Life Meaning and Death

Human beings think about the impact and inevitability of death throughout much of their lives. Most children understand by the ages of 5 to 7 that death is the irreversible ending of all life functions, and that it happens to all living beings. Adolescents fully comprehend the meaning of death, but they often believe that they are somehow immortal. As a result, they may engage in risky behavior, such as driving recklessly or smoking, with little thought of dangerous consequences.

Although most young and middle adults have gained a more realistic view of death through the death of some family members or friends, anxiety about death may be more likely to peak in middle adulthood. As people continue aging, they gradually learn to accept the eventual deaths of loved ones, as well as their own deaths. By later adulthood, most people come to accept—perhaps with some tranquility if they feel they have lived meaningfully—the inevitability of their own demise, which prompts them to live day by day and make the most of whatever time remains. If they do not feel they have lived meaningfully, older adults may react to impending death with feelings of bitterness or even passivity.

The concept of searching for meaning in life through death is one of the foundations of **existential psychology.** Existential psychologists like Rollo May believe that individuals must accept the inevitability of their own deaths and the deaths of loved ones; otherwise, they cannot fully embrace or find true meaning in life. This theory tracks with research that indicates that the more purpose and meaning that individuals see in their lives, the less they fear death. In contrast, the denial of death leads to **existential anxiety,** which can be a source of emotional troubles in daily life.

The Stages of Dying and Death

Perhaps the best-known pioneer in thanatology is Elisabeth Kubler-Ross, who after interviewing 200 terminally ill people proposed five stages of coming to terms with death. Upon learning of their own impending death, dying people's first reaction is often **denial,** in which they refuse to acknowledge the inevitable, perhaps believing a mistake has been made. They may seek other medical opinions and diagnoses or pretend that the situation will simply go away on its own. Gradually, as they realize that they are going to die, the terminally ill experience **anger** at having their lives end prematurely. They may become envious and resentful of those who will continue on, especially if they feel that their own life plans and dreams will go unfulfilled. Individuals who are dying will then attempt to **bargain,** often with God or another religious figure, and will promise to change or make amends or atone for their wrongdoings. When bargaining fails, they experience **depression** and hopelessness. During this stage, the terminally ill may mourn the loss of health that has already occurred, as well as the impending losses of family and plans. Finally, those dying learn to **accept** the inevitable, paving the way for a smoother transition both for themselves and loved ones.

Kubler-Ross pointed out that although the above five stages are typical, they are not absolute. Not all people progress predictably through all the stages, nor do people experience the stages in one particular order. Additionally, these stages do not necessarily represent the healthiest pattern for all individuals under all circumstances. Kubler-Ross and others also have noted that people whose loved ones are dying may progress through the same five stages as the dying person.

An individual who is not facing an immediate death has more time to adjust to the idea. In fact, dying can be a time of increased personal growth. The **life review,** or process of reminiscing, can help people examine the significance of their lives and prepare for death by making changes and finishing uncompleted tasks. Many dying individuals report that they are finally able to sort out who and what is the most important to them and are able to enjoy to the fullest what time remains. Many also report that dying is a time of religious awakening and transcendence.

Following the death of a loved one, survivors normally experience **bereavement,** or a change in status, as in the case of a spouse becoming a widow or widower. The behavioral response of the bereaved person is termed **mourning;** the emotional response is termed **grief.** People vary in their patterns of mourning and grief, both within and across cultures. People may also experience **anticipatory grief,** or feelings of loss and guilt, while the dying person is still alive.

Grieving typically begins with shock or disbelief, and is quickly followed by intense and frequent memories of the dead person. When those who are grieving finally attain resolution, or acceptance of the person's passing, they resume everyday activities and are able to move on with their lives.

People grieve in considerably different ways. Some adults are very vocal in their expressions of grief, while others prefer to be alone to quietly gather their thoughts and reflect on the loss of the loved one. Of course, cultural groups around the world handle grief according to their own customs. Egyptian mourners, for example, may cry loudly in public as a sign of grief, while Japanese mourners may talk quietly to the deceased person while kneeling in front of a home altar.

Dealing with Dying and Death

A variety of options are available for individuals seeking to cope with dying and death. **Grief therapy** counseling, and support groups can help individuals deal with their grief and bereavement. **Hospice,** which can occur at home or in a hospital or other institution, can provide care for dying persons and their families. Hospices are designed for terminally ill patients to live out their remaining days as independently, fully, and affordably as possible. **Death education** can also help by providing people with information on dying, legal issues, and various practical matters. Classes on death and dying are available at colleges, hospitals, and community centers. Many people take comfort in **bibliotherapy,** or reading books about dying, perhaps explaining the popularity of the life-after-life books. These testimonials detail the alleged journeys of people who were clinically dead into the afterlife before they were resuscitated.

Widowhood

Widowhood, or the disruption of marriage due to the death of the spouse, is a source of great emotional pain and stress. **Widows** (females whose spouse has died) and **widowers** (males whose spouse has died) may grieve and mourn their loss for years. Nearly 3 percent of men and 12 percent of women in all age groups in the United States are widowed. Among people age 75 and older, nearly 25 percent of men and 66 percent of women are widowed.

Widowhood is similar to divorce in that it signifies the end of a marriage, but widowhood differs from divorce in some important ways. Death is often an unexpected ending of a relatively happy, loving relationship, whereas divorce is usually the mutually agreed upon conclusion of a troubled relationship and the result of a long series of events. Death is also final, whereas many divorced persons maintain at least a superficial relationship with each other. Although people never really completely get over losing a loved one, most are ultimately able to cope.

How people deal with widowhood varies, especially by gender. Many men and women attempt to fill the void caused by their spouse's death by seeking out friendships or remarrying. Some people become more involved with their work or their children or grandchildren. Others volunteer for religious and charitable organizations. Still others enter counseling or find comfort within a local support group. Because they are usually socialized to be emotionally expressive, women may have an easier time dealing with the emotional issues associated with widowhood than men, but they often have a harder time financially. They also have to contend with youth-oriented social stigmas that are tied to widowhood—the myths that widows are used up and old, making it harder for women to remarry later, if they so choose. Widowers, on the other hand, are more likely to be depressed and attempt suicide than are widows.

Other Issues in Thanatology

Thanatologists are interested not only in such traditional subjects as grief and Kubler-Ross theories, but also in contemporary topics involving complicated moral and ethical issues. Debate over two of these issues—suicide and euthanasia—has stepped up as a result of changing state laws concerning physician-assisted suicide and technological advances, such as life-sustaining devices that patients are dependent upon.

Suicide

The majority of Americans view **suicide,** the deliberate termination of one's own life, as highly unfortunate, if not immoral. One conservative estimate is that 300,000 people attempt to kill themselves in the United States each year. Exact figures are hard to determine, and many presumed accidents may actually be disguised suicides or attempted suicides. Women outnumber men 3 to 1 in the number of attempted suicides, but men outnumber women 4 to 1 in the number of actual suicides. Men tend to use more lethal methods than women use when attempting suicide (for instance, guns instead of sleeping pills). The highest suicide rates are among older adult males.

While mostly an adult phenomenon, suicide occurs among children and adolescents, too. Although young children rarely succeed in committing suicide, some do. Each year, about 12,000 children ages 5 to 14 enter psychiatric hospitals for suicidal behavior. Suicide has increased among adolescents (especially males) by nearly 200 percent in recent years, yet the national average is still below that of middle-aged adults.

People attempt suicide for a number of reasons, including extreme negativity and pessimism about life, feelings of utter failure and hopelessness, and the desire to spare the world of their presence by no longer being in the way. Others attempt suicide to escape the agony and pain of a chronic or terminal illness. In contrast to nonsuicidal people who see a variety of acceptable options when faced with difficult situations, suicidal people see few or no options other than self-destruction.

Euthanasia

A very controversial issue, **euthanasia** (literally meaning, easy death or mercy killing) involves actively or passively assisting the death of a suffering person. **Active euthanasia** is the deliberate termination of life to eliminate pain. **Passive euthanasia** is the deliberate withdrawal or withholding of life-sustaining treatment (often termed, extraordinary measures) that may otherwise prolong the life of the dying person. Those individuals who want to avoid having extraordinary measures taken to keep them alive may draw up a **living will** that outlines their wishes in the case of terminal illness.

The issues of euthanasia in the United States have a long but especially complicated history due to modern advances in medicine. In
1828, New York enacted the first laws explicitly prohibiting assisted
suicide; many states followed New York's precedent shortly thereafter.
While deeply rooted in the law, states' rules against assisted suicide
have, in recent decades, been reexamined and typically reaffirmed.
Because so many North Americans today are likely to die from chronic
illnesses in hospitals, nursing facilities, and other long-term care institutions, the public has been particularly concerned with how best to
protect independence and dignity at the end of life.

A great deal of debate surrounds the subject of euthanasia, and
some states have introduced substantial changes in their laws as a result
of the considerations. For instance, many states now allow living wills
as well as the refusal or withdrawal of life-sustaining medical interventions. In 2000, Oregon's legalization of euthanasia took effect, and
California appears close to enacting similar legislation. Yet legislators
and voters generally continue to support laws that prohibit assisted
suicide, expressing concerns that voluntary euthanasia will become
involuntary euthanasia to control rising health-care costs in the elderly.
Objectors also express concern that assisted suicide will become a
primary treatment strategy that ignores first exploring other options.
Because some individuals see euthanasia as murder and others see it
as a humane means of helping the terminally ill to die with dignity, the
topic is likely to remain controversial for quite some time.

acceptance one of Elisabeth Kubler-Ross's stages of dying, in which the dying come to terms with their approaching death.

accommodation the altering of previous concepts in response to new information.

acne vulgaris a common, chronic skin disease, especially among adolescents and young adults, characterized by inflammation of the sebaceous apparatus, causing pimples on the face, back, and chest.

acquired immunodeficiency syndrome (AIDS) a condition in which acquired deficiency of certain leukocytes, especially T cells, results in a variety of infections, some forms of cancer, and the degeneration of the system: caused by a virus that infects T cells and is transmitted via body fluids, especially sexual secretions and blood.

active euthanasia the deliberate termination of life to eliminate pain.

activity theory sees a positive correlation between keeping active and aging well.

acuity acuteness; keenness, as of thought or vision.

adaptation a change in behavior to meet situational demands.

adolescence ages 12 to 19.

adolescent growth spurt a noticeable increase in height and weight during adolescence.

adult learners students age 25 or older.

affective disorder a mood disorder that causes a person to experience abnormally high and/or low feelings.

age clock the internal sense of timing of physical and social events that determines the various life stages through which adults pass.

ageism discrimination against people on the basis of age; specifically, discrimination against, and prejudicial stereotyping of, older people.

age–30 transition a stage in the novice phase of early adulthood; early adulthood ranging from ages 28 to 33.

aggression forceful, attacking behavior, either constructively self-assertive and self-protective or destructively hostile to others or to oneself.

Alzheimer's disease a progressive, irreversible disease characterized by degeneration of the brain cells and commonly leading to severe dementia.

ambidextrous able to use both hands with equal ease.

amniocentesis test the surgical procedure of inserting a hollow needle through the abdominal wall into the uterus of a pregnant woman and extracting amniotic fluid, which may be analyzed to determine the sex of the developing fetus or the presence of disease, genetic defects, and so on.

amnion the innermost membrane of the sac enclosing the embryo; it is filled with a watery fluid called amniotic fluid.

amniotic fluid the watery fluid that fills the amniotic sac and cushions the developing fetus against injury and shock and provides constant temperature in the amniotic sac.

amniotic sac a double-layered membrane formed from the fusion of the amnion and chorion; it encloses the embryo and is filled with amniotic fluid.

anal expulsive refers to traits in an adult—such as messiness and altruism—that may be regarded as unconscious psychic residues of the anal stage.

anal retentive refers to traits in an adult—such as orderliness, stinginess, strict adherence to schedules, and obstinancy—that may be regarded as unconscious psychic residues of the anal stage.

anal stage the second stage of psychosexual development, in which interest centers in excretory functions.

anger one of Elisabeth Kubler-Ross's stages of dying, in which the dying feel resentment or rage about their terminal illness.

anorexia nervosa an eating disorder, chiefly in young women, characterized by aversion to food and obsession with weight loss; manifested in self-induced starvation, excessive exercise, and so on.

anticipatory grief feelings of loss and guilt while the dying person is still alive.

anxiety disorder an abnormal state, characterized by a feeling of being powerless and unable to cope with threatening events, typically imaginary, and by physical tension, as shown by sweating, trembling, and so on.

applied intelligence practical IQ.

asexual not having sexual interests or abilities.

assimilation the application of previous concepts to new concepts.

assisted suicide suicide committed with the assistance of a physician by a person terminally ill or in unmanageable pain.

attachment the bond between a mother and child; also, the process whereby one individual seeks nearness to another individual.

authoritarian parents parents who demonstrate high parental control and low parental warmth when interacting with their children.

authoritative parents demonstrate appropriate levels of both parental control and parental warmth.

autonomy the ability to function independently without control by others.

babble the meaningless sounds babies make while learning to control their vocalizations.

bacteria tiny creatures making up a division (Bacteria) of microorganisms that are typically one-celled, have no chlorophyll, multiply by simple division, and can be seen only with a microscope: They occur in three main forms, spherical (cocci), rod-shaped (bacilli), and spiral (spirilla); some bacteria cause diseases such as pneumonia and anthrax, and others are necessary for fermentation, nitrogen fixation, and so on.

ballottement a type of pelvic examination in which a physician or nurse feels for a fetus in the uterus.

bargaining one of Elisabeth Kubler-Ross's stages of dying, in which the dying tries to bargain with God or another religious figure, promising to change, make amends, or atone for his or her wrongdoings in order to avoid death.

basic intelligence academic IQ.

bereavement to be left in a sad or lonely state, as by loss or death.

bibliotherapy dealing with death by reading books about dying.

bilingual using or capable of using two languages, especially with equal or nearly equal facility.

biopsychosocial perspective studies human development by examining the interaction of biological, psychological, and social factors.

bipolar disorder a psychotic disorder characterized by alternating periods of mania and mental depression; manic-depressive illness.

birth trauma injury incurred during birth.

bisexual sexually attracted to both sexes.

blastocyst an embryo at the stage of development in which it consists of usually one layer of cells around a central cavity, forming a hollow sphere.

blended families stepfamilies, in which new family units are made up of children from previous marriages.

borderline personality disorder a mental illness characterized by rapid shifts in the liking and hating of self and others.

breech presentation the delivery of a fetus presenting itself with its buttocks or feet first.

bulimia nervosa an eating disorder, chiefly in young women, characterized by the gorging of large quantities of food followed by purging, as through self-induced vomiting.

burnout a state of mental exhaustion characterized by feelings of helplessness and loss of control, as well as the inability to cope with or complete assigned work.

case study research research in which an investigator studies an individual who has a rare or unusual condition or who has responded favorably to a new treatment.

celibate abstaining from sexual intercourse.

cephalocaudal order the order in which fetal development occurs, beginning with the head and ending with the lower body and extremities.

cerebral hemisphere either of the two lateral halves of the cerebrum.

cesarean section (C-section) a surgical operation for delivering a baby by cutting through the mother's abdominal and uterine walls.

child development the maturation of children.

child molestation the sexual abuse of a child, which occurs when a teenager or adult entices or forces a child to participate in sexual activity.

child physical abuse the intentional infliction of pain, injury, and harm onto a child.

chloasma a skin discoloration on the face and chest, resulting from pregnancy, disease, malnutrition, and so on.

chorion the outermost of the two membranes that completely envelop a fetus.

chorionic villi small fingerlike projections in the placenta through which fetal blood circulates.

chorionic villus sampling a test for detecting genetic abnormalities, determining sex, and so on in a fetus: Tissue samples of chorionic villus are removed from the uterus.

chromosomes any of the microscopic rod-shaped bodies formed by the incorporation of the chromatin in a cell nucleus during mitosis and meiosis: They carry the genes that convey hereditary characteristics, and are constant in number for each species.

chronological age actual age.

classical conditioning (Pavlovian) a situation in which learning occurs by association when a stimulus that evokes a certain response becomes associated with a different stimulus that originally did not cause that response.

classification the ability to group according to features.

cognitive appraisal how people perceive and interpret the effects that situations have on them.

cohabitation to live together as husband and wife, especially when not legally married.

colostrum the first fluid, rich in protein, secreted by the mother's mammary glands for several days just after birth of the young.

companionate love a relationship in which two people are both committed and intimate, but not passionate.

conception when a sperm and egg unite, resulting in an embryo or fetus.

congenital defects birth defects existing as such at birth.

conservation the concept that physical properties remain constant even as appearance and form changes.

consummate love the ideal form of love in adulthood that involves three components: passion, intimacy, and commitment.

contextual intelligence the ability to apply intelligence practically, including taking into account social, cultural, and historical contexts.

continuing education classes taken by adults to expand their knowledge or skills for personal or work-related development.

continuity versus discontinuity debate examines the question of whether development is solely and evenly continuous, or whether it is marked by age-specific periods.

conventional morality characterized by conformity, helping others, obeying the law, and keeping order.

cooperative learning adult-supervised education that relies on peers interacting, sharing, planning, and supporting each other.

corpus callosum the bands of neural fibers connecting the two cerebral hemispheres.

corpus luteum during the early stages of pregnancy, a mass of yellow tissue formed in the ovary by a ruptured graafian follicle that has discharged its ovum: If the ovum is fertilized, this tissue secretes the hormone progesterone, needed to maintain pregnancy.

correlation the degree of relative correspondence, as between two sets of data.

cortex the higher areas of the brain, which are responsible for thinking and planning.

co-sleeping children sleeping in the same bed as their parents.

critical periods times of increased and favored sensitivity to particular aspects of development.

cross-cultural research research designed to reveal variations existing across different groups of people.

cross-gender behaviors behaviors stereotypical of the opposite sex.

cross-sectional study a study in which a number of different-age individuals with the same trait or characteristic of interest are studied at a single time.

cross-sequential study a study in which individuals in a cross-sectional sample are tested more than once over a specified period of time.

crowning the point during labor when the baby's head can be seen at the vaginal orifice.

crystallized intelligence the ability to use learned information collected throughout a life span.

culminating phase a phase of early adulthood that ranges from ages 33 to 45.

culture-fair IQ tests tests that are fair for all members in a culture.

culture-free IQ tests tests without cultural content.

death the permanent cessation of all life functions.

death education provides people with information on dying, legal issues, and various practical matters.

debrief to give information concerning research that has just been completed.

deception concealing the purpose and procedures of a study from participants.

deciduous teeth baby teeth; teeth that fall out at a certain stage of growth.

decision/commitment making the decision to commit to a relationship with another person.

delivery expelling the baby and placenta from the vagina.

dementia mental deterioration; a severe organic mental deficiency or impairment.

denial one of Elisabeth Kubler-Ross's stages of dying, in which the dying refuse to acknowledge their inevitable death, perhaps believing a mistake has been made.

dependent variable a variable whose value is determined by the value of another variable.

depression an emotional condition, either neurotic or psychotic, characterized by feelings of hopelessness, inadequacy, and so on; also one of Elisabeth Kubler-Ross's stages of dying.

depth perception the ability to see objects in perspective.

descriptive statistics statistics used for describing the characteristics of the population and subjects.

despair a loss of hope; Erik Erikson believed that those in late adulthood struggled with the fear that there is too little time to begin a new life course.

developmental psychology the scientific study of age-related changes throughout the human life span.

developmentalists researchers who study human development.

developmentally disabled persons who are slowed or delayed in development or progress, especially because of subnormal intellectual functioning and social skills.

diabetes mellitus a chronic form of diabetes involving an insulin deficiency and characterized by an excess of sugar in the blood and urine, and by hunger, thirst, and gradual loss of weight.

dialect the form or variety of a spoken language peculiar to a region, community, social group, occupational group, and so on.

didactic learning an educational method in which a teacher lectures to students.

discipline treatment that corrects or punishes and is intended to control or to establish habits of self-control.

disengagement theory views aging as a process of mutual withdrawal in which older adults voluntarily slow down by retiring, as expected by society.

distance education taking courses through alternative learning formats, such as intensive study classes conducted one weekend per month, telecourses provided over the television, or virtual classrooms set up on the Internet.

distortion when a subject does not respond honestly to questions.

distressor a negative event, such as a death or loss of a job, that is stressful.

divorce the legal and formal dissolution of a marriage.

early adult transition a stage in the novice phase of early adulthood, ranging from ages 17 to 22.

early adulthood ages 17 to 45.

early childhood ages 2 to 6.

early phase of labor the phase of labor that consists of mild, minute-long contractions that occur every 15 minutes.

eclampsia an attack of convulsions; specifically, a disorder that may occur late in pregnancy, characterized by convulsions, edema, and elevated blood pressure.

ectoderm the outer layer of cells of an embryo from which the nervous system, skin, hair, teeth, and so on are developed.

ectopic pregnancy a pregnancy with the fertilized ovum developing outside the uterus, as in a fallopian tube.

ego that part of the psyche that experiences the external world, or reality, through the senses, organizes the thought processes rationally, and governs action; it mediates between the impulses of the id, the demands of the environment, and the standards of the superego.

ego integrity maintaining one's sense of wholeness.

egocentric viewing everything in relation to oneself; self-centered.

elderly abuse the neglect and/or physical and emotional abuse of dependent elderly persons.

Electra complex the unconscious tendency of a daughter to be attached to her father and hostile toward her mother.

embryo an animal in the earliest stages of its development in the uterus or the egg, specifically, in humans, from conception to about the eighth week.

empathy the projection of one's own personality into the personality of another in order to understand the person better; ability to share in another's emotions, thoughts, or feelings.

empty-nest syndrome a form of mental depression said to be caused in parents by the loss felt when their children grow up and leave home.

endoderm the inner layer of cells of the embryo, from which the lining of the digestive tract, other internal organs, and certain glands are formed.

endometrium the inner lining of the uterus.

entering the adult world a stage in the novice phase of early adulthood, ranging from ages 22 to 28.

episiotomy incision of the perineum, often performed during childbirth to prevent injury to the vagina.

equilibrium Piaget's term for the basic process underlying the human ability to adapt; the search for balance between self and the world.

erogenous zone an area of the body that is particularly sensitive to sexual stimulation.

estrogen any of several female sex hormones that cause estrus; estrogen helps to stimulate enlargement of the reproductive organs and relaxation of associated ligaments, stimulate development of the uterine lining and mammary glands, and prevent contractions of the uterus.

ethical dilemma a situation in which a researcher must make a difficult moral decision.

eustressor a positive event, such as marriage or vacations, that is stressful.

euthanasia act or practice of causing death painlessly in order to end suffering: advocated by some as a way to deal with persons dying of incurable, painful diseases.

existential anxiety emotional troubles that arise from the denial of death.

existential psychology the search for meaning in life through the study of death.

experiential intelligence the ability to transfer learning effectively to new skills.

experimental research research based on, tested by, or having the nature of an experiment.

experimenter bias when researchers' expectations about what should or should not happen in a study sway the results.

extramarital affairs having sexual intercourse with someone other than one's spouse.

extraneous variable a variable unrelated to an experiment (such as room temperature or noise level) that may interfere with the results of the experiment.

fallopian tube either of two slender tubes that carry ova from the ovaries to the uterus.

family of origin the family one was born into or raised by.

fear a feeling of anxiety and agitation caused by the presence or nearness of danger, evil, pain, and so on.

fetal alcohol syndrome a condition affecting infants, characterized variously by mental retardation, heart defects, physical malformations, and so on and caused by excessive consumption of alcohol by the mother during pregnancy.

fetus the unborn young of an animal while still in the uterus or egg, especially in its later stages and specifically, in humans, from about the eighth week after conception until birth.

fimbria a fringe or border of hairs, fibers, and so on or a fringelike process, especially at the opening of an oviduct in mammals.

fine motor skills the use of small bodily movements, such as drawing or writing.

fixation an exaggerated preoccupation; obsession.

flagellum a whiplike part or process of some cells, especially of certain bacteria, protozoans, and so on, that is an organ of locomotion or produces a current in the surrounding fluid.

fluid intelligence the ability to think abstractly and deal with novel situations.

folkway any way of thinking, feeling, behaving, and so on common to members of the same social group.

formal operations according to Piaget, individuals enter this stage in adolescence as they gain the ability to classify and compare objects and ideas, systematically seek solutions to problems, and consider future possibilities.

fraternal twins two fetuses produced from separate eggs.

friendship a loving relationship characterized by intimacy, but not by passion or commitment.

frontal lobes lobes located in the front of the brain just under the skull, which are responsible for planning, reasoning, social judgment, and ethical decision making, among other functions.

full-term babies babies who arrive on or shortly before or after their due dates.

gay bashing attacks against homosexuals—either verbal or physical.

gender the fact or condition of being a male or a female human being, especially with regard to how this affects or determines a person's self-image, social status, goals, and so on.

gender identity an individual's personal sense of maleness or femaleness.

gender role outward expression of gender identity, according to cultural and social expectations.

gender schemas deeply embedded cognitive frameworks regarding what defines masculine and feminine.

gene any of the units occurring at specific points on the chromosomes, by which hereditary characters are transmitted and determined: Each is regarded as a particular state of organization of the chromatin in the chromosome, consisting primarily of DNA and protein.

generalize to formulate general principles or inferences from particulars.

generativity the desire to expand one's influence and commitment to family, society, and future generations.

genital stage adult or final stage of psychosexual development in which conflicts have been resolved, libidinal drives regulated, and character structure integrated.

gerontologists those who study the process of aging and of the problems of aged people.

gerontology the scientific study of the process of aging and of the problems of aged people.

gestation the act or period of carrying young in the uterus from conception to birth; pregnancy.

glial cells nervous system support cells surrounding neurons.

grief intense emotional suffering caused by loss, disaster, misfortune, and so on; acute sorrow; deep sadness.

grief therapy treatment that helps individuals deal with their grief and bereavement.

gross motor skills the use of large bodily movements, including running, jumping, hopping, turning, skipping, throwing, balancing, and dancing.

handedness ability in using one hand more skillfully than, and in preference to, the other.

hardiness resistance to stress.

heterosexual of or characterized by sexual desire for those of the opposite sex.

holophrase a single word that conveys complete ideas.

homophobia irrational hatred or fear of homosexuals or homosexuality.

homosexual of or characterized by sexual desire for those of the same sex as oneself.

hospice a homelike facility to provide supportive care for terminally ill patients.

human chorionic gonadotropin (HCG) the hormone that is secreted by the placenta early in pregnancy and which inhibits menstrual periods.

hyaluronidase an enzyme that inactivates hyaluronic acid by breaking down its polymeric structure, thus promoting the diffusion of substances through tissues: found in sperm cells, certain venoms and bacteria, and so on.

hypothesis an unproved theory, proposition, supposition, and so on, tentatively accepted to explain certain facts or to provide a basis for further investigation, argument, and so on.

hysterectomy the surgical removal of all or part of the uterus.

id that part of the psyche that is regarded as the reservoir of the instinctual drives and the source of psychic energy; it is dominated by the pleasure principle and irrational wishing, and its impulses are controlled through the development of the ego and superego.

identical triplets three fetuses produced from the same ovum.

identical twins two fetuses produced from the same ovum.

identification a mainly unconscious process by which a person formulates a mental image of another person and then thinks, feels, and acts in a way that resembles this image.

identity the condition or fact of being a specific person or thing; individuality.

identity crisis the condition of being uncertain of one's feelings about oneself, especially with regard to character, goals, and origins, occurring especially in adolescence as a result of growing up under disruptive, fast-changing conditions.

incest sexual activity between closely related persons of any age.

independent variable a variable whose value may be determined freely without reference to other variables.

indifferent parents parents who demonstrate low parental control and low warmth.

industry the feeling of social competence; according to Erikson, the primary developmental task of middle childhood is to attain industry.

infancy birth to age 1.

infant mortality the percentage of babies who die within the first year of life.

infatuation completely carried away by foolish or shallow love or affection.

inferential statistics statistics used for making predictions about the population.

infertile the inability to produce offspring because of some disorder of the reproductive system.

informed consent when a subject agrees to participate in a study based on disclosure of personal information.

initiative the ability to think and act without being urged; enterprise.

injunctions messages received during childhood.

intelligence the ability to learn or understand from experience; ability to acquire and retain knowledge; mental ability.

intelligence quotient (IQ) a number intended to indicate a person's level of intelligence: It is the mental age (as shown by intelligence tests) multiplied by 100 and divided by the chronological age.

interactional theory of homosexuality a theory stating that sexual orientation develops from a complex interaction of biological, psychological, and social factors.

interviewer bias an error in research that occurs when an interviewer's expectations or gestures influence a subject's responses.

intimacy the sense of warmth and closeness in a loving relationship, including the desire to help the partner, self-disclose, and keep him or her in one's life.

juvenile delinquency the breaking of the law by minors.

labor the process or period of childbirth; parturition; especially, the muscular contractions of giving birth.

Lamaze method a training program in natural childbirth, emphasizing breathing control and relaxation during labor together with the presence and encouraging assistance of a partner.

late adulthood those years that encompass age 65 and beyond, according to Daniel Levinson.

late phase of labor the phase of labor in which contractions become very painful, and the cervix dilates completely to 10 cm, or 4 inches.

lateralization the localization of assorted functions, competencies, and skills in either or both hemispheres.

learning the acquiring of knowledge or skill.

life review the process of reminiscing and examining the scope of one's life.

living will a document, legal in some states, directing that all measures to support life be ended if the signer should be dying of an incurable condition.

long-term memory a type of memory in which information is stored indefinitely.

longitudinal study a study in which the same individuals are studied repeatedly over a specified period of time.

low birthweight baby a baby born weighing less than 5½ pounds.

lunar month a four-week period of 28 days.

male climacteric male menopause.

marriage to be joined as husband and wife; united in wedlock.

memory the power, act, or process of recalling to mind facts previously learned or past experiences.

menarche the first menstrual period of a girl in puberty.

menopause the permanent cessation of menstruation, normally between the ages of 40 and 50, or the period during which this occurs; female climacteric, or change of life.

menstruate to have a menstrual period; undergo menstruation.

mental age an individual's degree of mental development measured in terms of the chronological age of the average individual of corresponding mental ability.

mesoderm the middle layer of cells of an embryo, from which the skeletal, reproductive, muscular, vascular, and connective tissues develop.

metacognition the awareness of one's own cognitive processes.

metamemory the ability to comprehend the nature of memory and predict how well one will remember something.

midcareer reassessment a reevaluation of one's career at midlife, which may lead to a career change.

middle childhood ages 7 to 11.

middle phase of labor that phase of labor in which contractions increase in strength and frequency, and the cervix dilates to at least 5 cm, or 2 inches.

midlife crisis the sense of uncertainty or anxiety about one's identity, values, relationships, and so on that some people experience in midlife.

midlife transition a change in lifestyle or career that some people may experience at midlife; also, a stage in the culminating phase of early adulthood, ranging from ages 40 to 45.

midwife a person whose work is helping women in childbirth.

miscarriage the natural expulsion of an embryo or fetus from the womb before it is sufficiently developed to survive.

mitochondria any of various very small, usually rodlike, structures found in the cytoplasm of eukaryotic cells and that serve as a center of intracellular enzyme activity that produces the ATP needed to power the cell.

mnemonic devices various devices that help, or are meant to help, the memory.

moral development and judgment the ability to reason about right and wrong.

mores formal rules of acceptable behavior that are considered conducive to the welfare of society and so, through general observance, develop the force of law, often becoming part of the formal legal code.

morning sickness a condition of nausea and vomiting, sometimes accompanied by dizziness, headache, and so on, that affects many women during the first months of pregnancy; it occurs most often in the morning.

motor skills the ability to move with intention.

mourning the actions or feelings of one who feels or expresses sorrow; specifically, the expression of grief at someone's death.

multi-infarct dementia dementia resulting from a stroke.

multiple pregnancy a pregnancy in which two or more eggs are fertilized, or a single fertilized egg divides into two or more zygotes.

mutuality synchronous (back-and-forth) interaction between individuals.

myelin sheaths a white, fatty material that surrounds, insulates, and increases the efficiency of neurons.

nature-versus-nurture debate arguments concerning the relative degree to which heredity and learning affect functioning.

neonatal period the first 4 weeks of life outside the womb.

neurons the structural and functional unit of the nervous system, consisting of the nerve cell body and all its processes, including an axon and one or more dendrites.

nocturnal emissions the release of semen during sleep (wet dreams).

nonviable fetus a fetus that is unable to live on its own.

norm a way of behaving typical of a certain group.

novice phase a phase of early adulthood, ranging from ages 17 to 33.

obesity being 20 percent or more above one's ideal weight.

object permanence the knowledge that out-of-sight objects still exist, learned by infants at around 9 months.

object-relations theory Melanie Klein's theory that the inner core of personality stems from the early relationship with the mother.

observational learning the process by which learning is achieved through observing and imitating others.

observational research research based on the observation of subjects in laboratory or natural settings rather than on experimentation or interviews.

Oedipus conflict the unconscious tendency of a child to be attached to the parent of the opposite sex and hostile toward the other parent. Its persistence in adult life results in neurotic disorders. Originally restricted to a son's attachment.

only child a child without siblings.

operant conditioning a form of conditioning in which the desired response, when it occurs, is reinforced by a stimulus.

oral stage the earliest stage of psychosexual development in which interest centers around sucking, feeding, and biting.

organic brain syndrome mental deterioration, also known as dementia.

ovulate to produce and discharge ova from the ovary.

ovum a mature female germ cell which, only after fertilization, develops into a zygote and then a fetus.

paranoia a mental disorder characterized by systematized delusions, as of grandeur or, especially, persecution; often, except in a schizophrenic state, occuring within an otherwise relatively intact personality.

parental control the degree to which parents are restrictive in their use of parenting techniques.

parental warmth the degree to which parents are loving, affectionate, and approving in their use of parenting techniques.

participant observation research that requires an observer to become a member of his or her subjects' community.

parturition the act of bringing forth young; childbirth.

passion intense feelings of physiological arousal and excitement.

passive euthanasia the deliberate withdrawal or withholding of life-sustaining treatment that may otherwise prolong the life of the dying person.

pedophilia an abnormal condition in which an adult has a sexual desire for children.

peer pressure to be forced or compelled to do something by one's peers.

perception the psychological process by which the human brain processes the sensory data collected by the sensory organs.

perineum the region of the body between the thighs, at the outlet of the pelvis; specifically, the small area between the anus and the vulva in the female or between the anus and the scrotum in the male.

permissive parents parents who demonstrate high parental warmth and low parental control when interacting with their children.

personality habitual patterns and qualities of behavior of any individual as expressed by physical and mental activities and attitudes; distinctive individual qualities.

petting sexual activities other than intercourse.

phallic stage designating or of the third stage of psychosexual development in which interest centers around the genital organs.

phenylketonuria (PKU) a genetic disorder of phenylalanine metabolism, which, if untreated, causes severe mental retardation in infants through the accumulation of toxic metabolic products.

physical development the biological changes that humans undergo as they age.

physical disability any physical defect, change, difficulty, or condition that has the potential to disrupt daily living.

physical intimacy mutual affection and sexual activity.

placenta a vascular organ that is connected to the embryo by the umbilical cord and that is discharged shortly after birth; the structure serves to provide nourishment for and eliminate wastes from the fetus.

placental lactogen a hormone produced by the placenta that prepares the mammary glands to secrete milk.

population a body of persons having qualities or characteristics in common.

positive reinforcement the rewarding of acceptable behaviors.

postconventional morality moral reasoning and behavior characterized by accepting the relative and changeable nature of rules and laws, and conscience-directed concern with human rights.

postformal thinking the objective use of practical common sense to deal with unclear problems.

postmature baby an infant who is born 2 or more weeks after its due date.

postpartum stage the period following childbirth.

preadolescence the period of childhood between ages 10 and 11.

preconventional morality moral reasoning and behavior based on rules and fear of punishment and nonempathetic self-interest.

prefrontal cortex the most anterior (front) portion of the frontal lobes; appears to be responsible for personality.

pregnancy the condition, quality, or period of having (an) offspring developing in the uterus.

prejudice suspicion, intolerance, or irrational hatred of other races, creeds, regions, occupations, and so on.

premature (preterm) birth a birth that occurs before a gestation of 37 weeks.

preoperational stage according to Piaget, the stage of cognitive development that occurs between ages 2 and 7.

presbycusis difficulty hearing high-pitched sounds.

presbyopia a form of farsightedness occurring after middle age, caused by a diminished elasticity of the crystalline lens.

primary sex characteristics any of the physical characteristics differentiating male and female individuals; directly responsible for reproduction.

productive language an ability to use the spoken or written word.

progesterone a hormone secreted by the corpus luteum, active in preparing the uterus for the reception and development of the fertilized ovum and the mammary glands for milk secretion.

promiscuity characterized by a lack of discrimination; specifically, engaging in sexual intercourse indiscriminately or with many persons.

prosocial behavior the capacity to help, cooperate, and share with others.

psychiatric disability a mental illness or psychological disturbance, causing a person to struggle with mild to incapacitating emotional problems and limitations that are often caused by either anxiety or affective disorders.

psycholinguists specialists in the study of language.

psychological intimacy the sharing of feelings and thoughts.

psychosexual development Freud's theory that children systematically move through oral, anal, phallic, and latency stages before reaching mature adult sexuality in the genital stage.

psychosocial of or pertaining to the psychological development of the individual in relation to his or her social environment.

puberty the stage of physical development when secondary sex characteristics develop and sexual reproduction first becomes possible: in common law, the age of puberty is generally fixed at fourteen for boys and twelve for girls.

punishment the infliction of some penalty on a wrongdoer.

qualitative research research in which information collected from respondents takes the form of verbal descriptions or direct observations of events.

quantitative research research in which information is collected from respondents and converted into numbers.

questionnaire a written or printed form used in gathering information on some subject or subjects, consisting of a set of questions to be submitted to one or more persons.

quickening the stage of pregnancy in which the movement of the fetus can be felt for the first time.

random sample a sample in which each member of a population has an equal chance of being chosen as a subject.

Raven's Progressive Matrices Test an IQ test that gauges the subject's ability to solve problems that are presented in unfamiliar designs.

receptive language an understanding of the spoken and written word.

reductionistic perspective studies human development by reducing complex phenomenon or events to a single cause.

reflex an involuntary action, as a sneeze, resulting from a stimulus that is carried by an afferent nerve to a nerve center and the response that is reflected along an efferent nerve to some muscle or gland.

refractory periods the waiting time before men can regain an erection after they have ejaculated.

reliable that which can be relied on; dependable; trustworthy; in testing, provides consistent results when administered on different occasions.

representational thought symbolic thought, which children begin exhibiting around ages 18 to 24 months.

Rh factor incompatibility group of antigens, determined by heredity and usually present in human red blood cells, that may cause hemolytic reactions during pregnancy or after transfusion of blood containing this factor into someone lacking it.

rubella a mild, infectious, communicable virus disease, characterized by swollen glands, especially of the back of the head and neck, and small red spots on the skin; German measles.

sample a selected segment of a population studied to gain knowledge of the whole.

schemas Piaget's term for innate thinking processes.

scientific method a systematic approach to researching questions and problems through objective and accurate observation, collection and analysis of data, direct experimentation, and replication of these procedures.

secondary sexual characteristic any of the physical characteristics that differentiate male and female individuals, as distribution of hair or fat on the body, breast and muscle development, deepening of the voice, and so on, that are not directly related to reproduction and usually appear at puberty.

selective attention the ability to focus or concentrate closely on something.

self-concept one's conception of oneself and one's own identity, abilities, worth, and so on.

self-esteem belief in oneself; self-respect.

senile showing the marked deterioration often accompanying old age, especially mental impairment characterized by confusion, memory loss, and so on.

sensation the power or process of receiving conscious sense impressions through direct stimulation of the bodily organism; an immediate reaction to external stimulation of a sense organ; conscious feeling or sense impression.

sensorimotor of or pertaining to motor responses initiated by sensory stimulation.

sensorimotor stage according to Piaget, from birth to age 2, infants and toddlers learn by doing: looking, hearing, touching, grasping, and sucking.

sensory memory a form of memory in which information is retained for less than 1 second.

sensory organs specialized structures of the body containing sensory receptors that receive stimuli from the environment.

sensory receptors convert environmental energy into nervous-system signals that the brain can understand and interpret.

separation anxiety distress at the prospect of being left alone in an unfamiliar place or being separated from a familiar person.

serial ordering the ability to group according to logical progression.

settling down a stage in the culminating phase of early adulthood, ranging from ages 33 to 40.

sex role the quality of being male or female, based on anatomy.

sexual latency inactive sexual interest.

sexual orientation an individual's sexual, emotional, romantic, and affectionate attraction to members of the same sex, the other sex, or both.

short-term memory a form of memory in which information is retained for less than 30 seconds.

size and shape constancy the consistent size and shape of objects.

social cognition experiential knowledge and understanding of society and the rules of social behavior.

social deprivation the absence of attachment.

social inferences assumptions about the nature of social relationships, processes, and others' feelings.

social intimacy having the same friends and enjoying the same types of recreation.

socializing agents those influences that teach and reinforce society's rules and norms.

stable identity the concept that one's self remains consistent even when circumstances change.

stage theories of development theories that suggest that people go through a series of discrete stages, each of which is characterized by at least one task that an individual must accomplish before progressing to the next stage.

stagnation a state of self-absorption, self-indulgence, and invalidism that middle adults may experience if they fail to develop generativity.

Stanford-Binet Intelligence Scale a popular IQ test.

state a set of circumstances or attributes characterizing a person or thing at a given time; way or form of being; condition.

statistics facts or data of a numerical kind, assembled, classified, and tabulated so as to present significant information about a given subject.

stillbirth the birth of a dead fetus after 20 weeks.

stranger anxiety distress in the presence of unfamiliar people.

stress mental or physical tension or strain.

subcortical the lower areas of the brain, which are responsible for basic life functions. *processing/relaying neural impulses between different parts of brain.*

subjects members of a population who participate in a study.

sudden infant death syndrome (SIDS) the sudden death of an apparently healthy infant, of unknown cause but believed to be related to some faulty mechanism in respiration control.

suicide the act of killing oneself intentionally.

superego that part of the psyche that is critical of the self or ego and enforces moral standards: at an unconscious level it blocks unacceptable impulses of the id.

survey research research that involves interviewing or administering questionnaires to large numbers of people.

telegraphic speech speech of 1 to 2-year-olds in which two or more meaningful words are put together to form brief sentences.

teratogen an agent, as a chemical, disease, and so on, that causes malformation of a fetus.

tetrahydrocannabinol (THC) the hallucinatory chemical that is the principal and most active ingredient in marijuana.

thanatologists those who examine all aspects of death, including biological, psychological, and social issues.

thanatology the study of death, especially of the medical, psychological, and social problems associated with dying.

theory an integrated set of statements that explain various phenomena.

theory of mind an awareness and understanding of others' states of mind and accompanying actions.

toddlerhood ages 1 to 2.

trait a distinguishing quality or characteristic, as of personality.

triarchic theory of intelligence a theory stating that intelligence consists of three factors: information-processing skills, context, and experience.

trimester a period or term of three calendar months (13 weeks).

trophoblast a layer of nutritive ectoderm outside the blastoderm, by which the fertilized ovum is attached to the uterine wall and the developing embryo receives its nourishment.

ultrasound examination (sonogram) an examination that involves bouncing high frequency sound waves off the fetus and transforming the bounced waves into visual images.

umbilical cord a tough, cordlike structure connecting the navel of a fetus to the placenta and serving to supply nourishment to, and remove waste from, the fetus.

unemployment the state of being unemployed; lack of employment.

unipolar depression a mood disorder marked by feelings of self-blame, sadness, guilt, and apathy.

uterus a hollow, muscular organ of female mammals in which the ovum is deposited and the embryo and fetus are developed; womb.

valid well-grounded on principles or evidence; able to withstand criticism or objection, as an argument; sound; in testing, describes a test that measures what it purports to measure.

variable anything changeable; especially, a quality or quantity that varies or may vary.

viable fetus a fetus that is able to live outside of the uterus.

villi any of numerous hairlike or fingerlike vascular processes on certain mucous membranes of the body, as of the small intestine, serving to secrete mucus, absorb fats, and so on; or of the chorion in the mammalian placenta, serving in the exchange of food materials, and so on between the mother and the fetus.

viruses noncellular, microscopic particles that replicate themselves within invaded cells.

volunteer bias an error in research that occurs when a sample of volunteers is not representative of the general population.i

Wechsler Intelligence Scale for Children (WISC) a popular IQ test.

widow a woman who has outlived the man to whom she was married at the time of his death; especially, such a woman who has not remarried.

widower a man who has outlived the woman to whom he was married at the time of her death; especially, such a man who has not remarried.

widowhood the disruption of marriage due to the death of the spouse.

wisdom expert and practical knowledge based on life experience.

workaholism addiction to work.

zona pellucida the gelatinous covering of the egg.

zygote a cell formed by the union of male and female gametes; fertilized egg cell before cleavage.

Notes

Does Kohlberg assign ages?

Notes

Notes